To Jake, May God bless you

EARL'S PEARLS

ON

ENJOYING EXCELLENCE

By

Dr. Earl L. Suttle

and

Dr. John R. Hubbard

30 Pearls of Wisdom
(one for each day of the month)

VICTORY INTERNATIONAL PUBLISHERS
Atlanta • Georgia

© 2003 Victory International Publishers
Atlanta, Georgia
All Rights Reserved.

Published by Victory International Publishers
920 Renaissance Way
Roswell, Georgia 30076
www.earlsuttle.com.

This book was set in Adobe Caslon
Cover Design and Composition by Jonathan Pennell

Library of Congress Catalog Number: Applied For
        Suttle. Earl, and Hubbard. John R.
Earl's Pearls on Enjoying Excellence

        ISBN: 1-9729971-0-5 (Soft cover)
        ISBN: 1-9729971-1-3 (Hard cover)

First Edition
10   9   8   7   6   5
Printed in the United States of America

About the Authors

EARL L. SUTTLE, Ph.D.

"Empowerment through education and enthusiasm" is the mission statement of Earl Suttle, who is trained as a clinical psychologist and is an internationally recognized keynote speaker, seminar leader, and management consultant. He is the Founder and President of Three E Corporation, an international leadership consulting and training corporation based in the Atlanta, Georgia area. Earl Suttle annually delivers over 75 energizing and entertaining presentations in the US and South Africa. He is also the author of several motivational audiotapes on leadership and personal development. His subject matter is versatile; seminars include topics such as leadership, stress management, coping with change, and embracing diversity and inclusion in the workplace. He has conducted keynote addresses and seminars for AFLAC, The Coca-Cola Company, American Express, Kimberly-Clark Corporation, U.S. Postal Service, Kraft Foods, The Hartford Insurance Group, Georgia Department of Labor, Cobb Energy, Anheuser-Busch Companies, Inc., the University of Miami, the University of Georgia, and many more. Earl is also a consultant to the National Basketball Association and National Football League where he works with players on a personal level. He is married to Felicia Mabuza-Suttle, South Africa's top-rated television talk-show host, and is the proud father of one son Darron and two daughters, Lindi and Zani. As a motivational speaker, Earl is available to do keynote speaking at conventions, companies, various associations, school systems, and churches.

Earl can be reached via:
    phone: 770-650-0399
    e-mail: earl@earlsuttle.com or info@victoryvip.com
    website: www.earlsuttle.com or www.victoryvip.com

* * * *

JOHN R. HUBBARD, Ph.D., M.D.

John R. Hubbard, Ph.D., M.D. is a physician (M.D. from the Medical College of Virginia), scientist (Ph.D. in Biochemistry), board certified psychiatrist (residency training from the University of Virginia School of Medicine), and board certified addiction specialist. He has previously published six books (including *Handbook of Stress Medicine and Substance Abuse in the Mentally and Physically Disabled*), over seventy manuscripts, review articles or book chapters, and more than thirty scientific or clinical research abstracts. His expertise and publications are in such diverse areas as stress, addiction, psychiatry, general medicine, chronic pain, and hormones. Dr. Hubbard has been the Director of the Outpatient Addiction Program at Vanderbilt University Medical Center and has worked with professional athletes in the National Football League's Substance Abuse Program. As a third year resident in psychiatry he was awarded the prestigious Laughlin Fellowship by the American College of Psychiatrists for "outstanding leadership and significant achievements as a resident in psychiatry." Dr. Hubbard is currently in a group private practice, and has been a medical school professor at such distinguished universities as Vanderbilt University School of Medicine, the University of Virginia School of Medicine, the Medical College of Virginia, and Harvard Medical School. Dr. John Hubbard is married to Dr. Suzanne W. Hubbard (a dentist, who is currently the Director of Dental Health Services for the State of Tennessee) and has two wonderful daughters, Tara and Erin.

Acknowledgments

WE WOULD LIKE TO THANK the countless people who have been mentors, coaches, friends, and special teachers to us. Although the list below may seem rather long to some readers, our concern is that we have left out many other important people. To those people, we thank you now and ask for your understanding.

DR. JOHN HUBBARD would like to give his special thanks to:

Dr. Suzanne W. Hubbard—my loving wife, who more than anyone in the world has inspired, encouraged, and motivated me to be my best. Sue's ability through the years to be a nurse, dentist, and most recently Director of a state dental health service while still being a great mother and wonderful wife is an inspiration to all who know her. My love and respect for her is boundless and everlasting.

Tara M. Reid and Erin A. Hubbard—my loving daughters, who have shown me unlimited love and confidence. Both Tara and Erin give my wife Suzanne and me great memories every day of our lives. We are so thankful that each has been blessed with good Christian men (Lt. Aaron Reid and Thomas "Trey" Coke) to share their lives.

Arline D. Hubbard—my loving mother, who told me each morning (when I was a child) to be "good, kind and careful." This is still good advice. I also thank my mother for the great pride and confidence she has in me.

Erwin L. Hubbard—my loving father, who taught me to stay active and not to let age alone keep me from enjoying athletics and other activities. I also thank my father for the great pride and confidence he has in me.

Nancy, Sandra, Scott, Tom, Don, Aaron, Elaine, Jim, and Marie—my loving brothers and sisters, who taught me much about the uniqueness and special gifts of each individual. Growing up in a large family was fun and taught me a great deal about how to play and work with other people.

John C. Neunan—my lifelong friend, for being part of my life despite time and distance. Everyone has one special lifelong friend and for me, I'm stuck with John. (Just kidding, John!)

Guy and Gay Holloway—my spiritual teachers, for teaching me about true faith, God's love and God's plan for our salvation. I owe them more gratitude than I could ever express.

Dr. Earl Suttle—my co-author, for his wonderful friendship, generosiy and for planning and dreaming with me about this book and other projects.

Dr. Voshell (my childhood orthopedic surgeon)—who taught me patience by not operating on my degenerative hips when I was a child (despite the advice of other surgeons who wanted to do so). My legs healed on their own and his conservative approach has allowed me to enjoy sports and other vigorous activities to this day.

Mr. Frazier—my 8th-grade teacher, for expressing such great confidence in me. He was the first person (outside of my family) to make me feel that I could achieve whatever I put my mind to.

Joseph P. Liberti, Ph.D.—my Ph.D. mentor, who taught me passion for my work, and how to critically analyze data and ideas.

Mohammed Kalimi, Ph.D.—my post-doctoral mentor, who showed me great personal kindness and how to enhance the efficiency and productivity in my work.

Edward A. Workman, M.D., Ed.D.—a friend and medical colleague, who has taught me a great deal about forensic medicine, use of computer technology in clinical and academic medicine, and care of chronic pain patients.

Kelly Moles, M.D.—a professor of psychiatry at the University of Virginia School of Medicine, whose style of insightful, practical and compassionate clinical psychiatry has been my model of clinical care.

* * * *

Dr. EARL L. SUTTLE would like to personally thank his mentors and friends, including:

Felicia Mabuza-Suttle—my wife, for her unwavering love, faith, and incredible patience in sticking it out with me through the hard times in our lives.

Sarah Grant and Charlie Rowe—my friends, who are responsible for me and my wife, Felicia, meeting each other.

Frances Pryor—my mother, whose motherly love brought the best out of me and always encouraged me to stay close to God.

Wilma and Sammie Randolph—my godparents, who over the years have been a source of encouragement to learn to take "one day at a time" and sometimes one minute at a time.

James Suttle—my father, who taught me the benefits of playing sports and how it would someday get me "out of the ghetto."

Darron, Lindi and Zani—my children, whose love and support over the years have sustained me to be a role model to them.

Dr. John Hubbard—my friend, for his encouragement and persistence to co-author and complete this book.

Fahad Nahi, Max Walker, Simon and Margie Sagonda—my friends, who helped me "keep my focus when I got off focus" and who have been there when I needed them.

Willie Jolley—my speaker mentor, who inspired me to pursue my dream as a speaker after hearing him speak at a Georgia Speakers Association meeting.

Dr. Lloyd Baccus—my mentor, who helped get me into a great career opportunity that has changed my life.

Dr. Herb Martin—my friend, who taught me that friendships need to be kept alive.

Stephanie Carmical—my friend, who taught me the true joy of laughter and putting family first.

Tom "Satch" Sanders—my sports hero, who taught me that team play is more important than individual glory.

* * * *

The writers of this book take sole responsibility for its contents.

The authors wish to thank Sheila Stamps and Diana Suttle for their talents, time, and availability in the preparation of this manuscript. Without them this work could not have been done. The authors also wish to thank our manuscript reviewers for their comments and suggestions; the reviewers include:

T. Gerald Faircloth

Carol Hacker

Rich Harrington (Textbook Writers Associates, Inc.)

Dr. J. LaValle Ingram

John C. Neunan

Most of all, we both thank God the Father and our Lord and Savior Jesus Christ, for everything!

Table of Contents

A S YOU GLANCE OVER the Table of Contents of our 30 Pearls, say out loud 10 times, "I will follow through with reading and getting the most I can from these Pearls." One of the most difficult things for people to do in life is to follow through on their intentions. John Wright, a former NFL football player, often lectures NFL rookies on the need to follow through. In his inspiring presentations, he states that one of the biggest weakness of human beings is the lack of follow-through on what they really intend to do in life. He cites statistics taken from Columbia University research study, which highlights the following:

- Less than 10% of all books purchased are read past the first chapter.
- Of the people who sign up for a health club, some will never go and the vast majority will quit within 3 months.
- Less than 50% of heart attack victims follow through with recommendations to change their lifestyle.
- About 40% of smoke alarms don't have effective batteries.
- For marriages in 1990 or later, the divorce rate is about 67%.

Wright also noted that in 2001, Blockbuster received $750,000,000 in late fees. A good chunk of that money was from us! (Dr. Hubbard keeps waiting for a wing at his local blockbuster to be named in his honor.) It has been said that the average number of pages read in most books is only 18 pages. So, our point here is, if you successfully make it through the third Pearl of this book you are already separating yourself from the pack. If you read the entire book then you are very special and will reap the rewards earned. We believe that any one of these Pearls, put into action, can CHANGE YOUR LIFE.

So say this affirmation out loud ten times, "I am following through with my intention to read each Pearl in this book. I do this for me." Now, notice what is happening in your mind or body.

CONTENTS

Preface

"The secret joy of work is contained in one word...Excellence."
—Pearl Buck

S A MOTIVATIONAL SPEAKER and executive coach, Dr. Earl Suttle has dedicated his career to motivating and coaching corporate executives, professional athletes, and many others to make changes towards greater success and excellence. Likewise, Dr. John Hubbard (as a physician, addiction specialist, medical school professor, and psychiatrist) has helped the lives of numerous patients, medical students, professional athletes, and others to achieve their goals and ambitions. In this book, Dr. Earl Suttle and Dr. John Hubbard combine their knowledge, talents, and experience to help readers move towards excellence and living the life they love. Trying to achieve excellence means consciously stepping back and re-examining who you are, what you do, how you do it, and where you are going. It also means taking personal responsibility for your life and consistently following through on your plans by taking actions that are needed for personal growth and fulfillment. Approaching life with high levels of self-discipline, enthusiasm, faith, passion, direction, and bulldog determination is the major theme of this book. These attributes and others (which we call "Pearls") will lead you to greater self-satisfaction, more opportunities, greater success, and more power to impact in a positive way the lives of others.

We do not believe that excellence and success are necessarily the same. Excellence is more than success alone. After all, success (in the worldly sense) can be achieved by both honorable and dishonorable means. People can be "successful" but very self-centered or dishonest. The many recent scandals involving corporate executives who made tens of millions at the expense of their stockholders and employees illustrate this point very well. Thus, success per se does not always bring true joy, self-satisfaction, or contributions to the world. You can probably think of people (certain work colleagues, celebrities, classmates, neighbors, or perhaps even family members) who are "successful" by outward standards but do not embody true joy and excellence. They may "get to the top" but ignore the people they step on to get there. These are people who do not care if what they do is right or wrong. They care only about themselves and about winning. Others may find success in certain parts of their lives, such as professional success, but falter in other important areas such as their health, marriage, and family. Balance in life is therefore another area that everyone must frequently re-examine and make adjustments as they are needed. A person's body, mind, and spirit must be in harmony if he or she is to optimize the blessings of life.

Our intention in writing this book is not only to move you towards excellence, but more importantly, to help you enjoy the process of getting there. At the same time we want to help you explore weaknesses in your thinking which prevent you from taking full control over your life. There are no "magic bullets" to achieving excellence, except perhaps the determination to achieve it. But the Pearls we present in this book are tried and true. They are concepts that have inspired people for centuries and are used by millions of outstanding people every day. The information and ideas in this book are gathered from a vast array of sources over many years of experience and from both formal and informal education. To the best of our ability, we have tried to give credit to specific sources of information and have provided a bibliography of some of the excellent books and other resources that have inspired us over the years.

This book is primarily about simple and practical ideas. But do not let that fool you! While ideas are not physical objects that can be picked up and held like money, they are real and very *powerful*. Both good and bad ideas have changed peoples' lives and even changed the history of the world. They can bring people down, or they can build people up. Think about the powerful influence ideas have had on the world and you will understand the true power of ideas. For example, Gandhi's idea of peacefully freeing India from the British Empire changed the course of history of one of the largest nations in the world. Hitler had a perverse idea of ruling an Aryan-dominated world. It was an exciting idea to a few greedy people, but it hurt or destroyed countless lives. Great ideas have led to the discovery of life-saving antibiotics, uncovered the human genome, enhanced religious faith, and helped create new countries, including the United States of America (USA). Remember, the USA was originally only a dream in the 1700's. It started out as an exciting (and dangerous) idea of a few inspired and determined men and women. Today, over two hundred years later, millions of Americans benefit from their idea of a free and united nation. So remember, IDEAS are POWERFUL.

However, for the Pearls in this book to change your life, you must put them into action!

Ideas are therefore worth considering and reconsidering. You may get one good idea from this book, or many. Either way can make a huge difference in your life. Sometimes just one good idea, put into action, can turn your life around. You may get one idea that will lead to a job promotion, help you make a best friend, re-ignite your marriage, or save you from drug abuse or bankruptcy. *However, for the Pearls in this book to change your life, you must put them into action!* You must develop the good habits that we bring to light in this book. Just reading them will make little difference. Instead, you can use this book like a workbook to help you to grow and achieve your dreams. Remember the "slight edge principle" of W. Clement Stone: "There is little difference between people. But a little difference makes a big difference." Most races are won by only inches! Often a person may get a job over another applicant only by the smallest of margins. This book is designed to give YOU that winning edge.

WARNING: Once you get started reading these Pearls, you will be tempted to take this book and read it while stuck in traffic or while you are going to work. But please don't read this book while driving your car. A better suggestion would be for you to take this book with you and put it in your purse or briefcase. Usually there are at least 1 or 2 hours per day of downtime available for reading. We also urge you not to loan this book to another person, because chances are they won't return it. Read it when no one is looking. Of course, you could always buy two books just in case you have a son, daughter and/or friend who really could benefit from reading it. We don't mind. Our last suggestion is to avoid leaving this book unattended because once a person sees this book, it's gone forever!

So take your time as you read this book. Perhaps read and put into action just one Pearl a day for the next month. You may wish to read the Pearls in the order given or go directly to a specific Pearl you need that day. At the end of each Pearl we provide specific ideas to try and specific affirmations to say. We also ask that you write down (space is provided) the most important points that you learned from each Pearl to help solidify important concepts in your mind.

After you have completed this book, pick it up again in a month or two and see how you are doing. Have you acquired the passion and discipline to put into practice the things that you intended to do? Ask your spouse and close friends if they see changes in you. If so, fantastic! If not, boy have you screwed up because there is gold in here! Remember, this book can become your toolbox to success and greater happiness.

Mission Statement

THE MISSION OF THIS BOOK is to help the readers develop attitudes, faith, skills, discipline, passion, and perseverance to enhance their lives. When all is said and done, we want you to remember this simple mnemonic: "TAP." TAP stands for TRUST (in God, yourself, your family, and others). Next comes ATTITUDE. The bottom line with attitude is to be a positive thinking person instead of a victim. "A" is also for ACTION, because no good intention is helpful without appropriate action. Finally, the "P" stands for PASSION and PERSEVERANCE. If you put passion in what you do, you will do it better and have more fun. People will enjoy being with you. And finally, whatever you put your heart and mind to do, have the perseverance to finish it.

Who or what can stop you if you use the "TAP Principle"? So next time you have a problem, tap your head with your finger or tap your pencil on the table and remember:

TAP
_____

1. **T**RUST

2. **A**TTITUDE & ACTION

3. **P**ASSION & PERSEVERANCE!

Dr. John R. Hubbard and Dr. Earl Suttle

PEARL # 1

Taking Responsibility Sets You Free

"The greatest ability is to take responsibility."
—**Jack Canfeild**

"The buck stops here."
—**Harry S Truman**

"Happiness depends upon ourselves."
—**Aristotle**

* * * *

TAKING PERSONAL RESPONSIBILITY for your life is a vital first step towards contentment, happiness, and success. It is also a good way to develop greater self-esteem. *It may sound strange, but taking responsibility SETS YOU FREE!* You may ask, how can this be? Doesn't taking responsibility mean taking on more pressure, guilt, and stress? The answer is NO. When you chronically blame other people, the economy, society, the weather, or anything else for your problems the

It may sound strange, but taking responsibility SETS YOU FREE!

internal message you tell yourself is that you are a VICTIM. You tell yourself that you are a slave to circumstances and can do little about it. Feeling like a victim causes you to lose your energy and the power you need to move forward. Blaming others assigns to others the responsibility for change, and that is hard to control. It takes you off the hook, but it also hinders your personal growth and development.

When you take responsibility, you feel more in control and it accelerates your ability to find solutions. You become more creative, feel more powerful, and you have more fun. For those areas of your life that are truly not possible to control (such as the death of a loved one), you may have to learn greater acceptance. In those situations, we suggest that you look to your faith and understand that God (or whatever name you use for the Creator) is ultimately in control and will one day set all things right. The Serenity Prayer is a useful tool to help you find peace. The Serenity Prayer says, "God, grant me the serenity to accept the things I cannot change, the courage to change the things I can, and the wisdom to know the difference" (Reinhold Neibuhr, 1926).

So where does taking greater responsibility begin? Most importantly you must try to gain control of your attitude and your reaction to life's stresses. Decide to develop a positive attitude and commit to always doing what is right in the long run. Do not trade in deep-seated happiness for momentary pleasures. You know what is right in your heart, and if you follow it, you will be at peace. Doing right makes taking responsibility much easier. If you want to take responsibility but don't know which way to turn, ask yourself, "What is the right thing to do?" Your heart will let you know.

When you find yourself blaming someone else (or something else), stop for a moment, make a U-turn, stand up, and take responsibility. "Press the delete button as you do with your computer," says Joyce Rennolds, an outstanding motivational speaker on prosperity. You will find that it not only feels good to press the delete button in your mind but it ignites a shift of energy within you. It will make you feel like the true adult and leader that you are. You will no longer feel like you are pushed around by bad luck and circumstances. By taking responsibility, you won't have to worry if someone else will blame you, because you beat him or her to it!

In our line of work, we see many people with all sorts of personal and emotional problems. Those who do not take responsibility for their lives tend to be chronically unhappy and usually walk around with a low level of energy in their emotional tank. These people have what might be called a "victimization persona." Who wants to be a victim? Actually, it appears that a lot of people do if you listen to what they say and how they behave. There is an often told story about a man sitting in a chair and screaming out loud in pain. A friend ran over to him and asked, "What's wrong?"

The man declared, "I am sitting on a nail."

His friend asked, "Why don't you get up?"

The man replied, "Oh, I'll get used to it."

Some people would rather complain than take personal responsibility to solve their problems. We know there are times when your car was hit by a bad driver or you were cheated by someone. No doubt bad things happen to you as they do to everyone. What we are warning against is taking a victimization approach to life. Complaining, whining, and accusing others are bad habits that some people develop to an excessive degree. It is important to change those bad habits into the better habit of taking responsibility.

Take responsibility for your **health**. It is up to you if you want to lose weight, increase your fitness, or stop risky behaviors such as smoking. Great health gives you more energy for better performance. Don't expect anyone else to get you up in the morning to go jogging or drag you to the gym. Develop a regular exercise program. It is one of the best habits you can have. If you do something physical, you have started out your day with a "victory." Lowell Jackson walks with Earl Suttle every morning. Each time he sees Earl from a distance he yells with hands up, "It's a victory." They both smile.

Earl began his brisk walking routine about ten years ago when he was diagnosed with diabetes. His health nurse recommended that he start to do brisk walking along with dieting. Earl recalls starting his walking routine around his neighborhood and many times would return only after walking a few blocks. Each time he came home, his daughter Lindi would say, "Daddy, you didn't do much." He soon realized she had been checking on him. Several months later Earl became more committed to walking long distances. Earl recalls his daughter driving by him one morning and saying, "Daddy, I'm really proud of you." They both smiled. As parents we often forget that our children are watching us all the time. Being a good example by exercising regularly is therefore important for both you and your children.

If you are starting from ground zero, try just going on a walk one to two times a week. Then work your way up. It helps put more oxygen into the lungs and is a great method for reducing your stress. More and more data shows the tremendous benefit of brisk walking for thirty minutes at least five days a week. If you are married, walk with your spouse. It is a good way to exercise, communicate, and relax together. Believe us when we say that NATURE will hold

YOU responsible for your health. It is you who must try to defend against heart disease, obesity, cancer, and age-related complications. Better health gives you more energy to do your work and enjoy many other aspects of your life. There is no telling Mother Nature, "My poor heath was their fault!"

Take responsibility at **work**. There is an old saying, "It is not the hours you put in at work, but what you put *into* those hours." In addition to hurting yourself when you avoid taking responsibility at work, you will appear immature and may even harm your coworkers. "It was her fault." "It was their fault." "Someone else should have done it." "That's not my job." How does that sound to you? When your coworkers find out what you said about them, what happens? They feel hurt and develop an "attitude" (as the old saying goes). They will get mad, frustrated, and resentful. The workplace becomes less pleasant or perhaps hostile. If you take responsibility for a problem at work what will happen? Suddenly, you will be a greater asset to your employer. You will gain more respect from your coworkers and you will have greater respect for yourself. Coworkers may even feel that they "owe you one." Your boss will also learn that you can be trusted. You will become a leader. As a leader, ask yourself, "Do I bring out the best in others with whom I work?" If not, ask, "How can I improve in this area?"

An excellent example of someone who shows great responsibility is Dr. Suzanne Hubbard, a public health dentist and wife of coauthor Dr. John Hubbard. Improving the dental health of poor children is more than a job to her—it is a mission. Dr. Suzanne Hubbard has always had a passion for children. At every job level, she has not only done the work expected of her extremely well, but also did whatever was needed to make quality dental care available to poor children. For example, when equipment would break down or water lines burst in the field, she would get things fixed as fast as possible even if she had to do it herself. She would do it because she truly wanted to get the children their care. Whether it meant crawling under a mobile dental van in the freezing cold or forcing less motivated people to do their job, she did it. While to some this may seem the obvious thing to do, it is not. You don't have to look hard to see that many other people in similarly salaried positions can't wait for an excuse to stop or slow the work down.

When conducting staff evaluations, Dr. Suzanne Hubbard is known for giving honest assessments, rather than "easy-way-out" grades (i.e., looking the other way so that no one complains). When people do their jobs correctly, no one is happier than Suzanne. Giving out less than perfect or even poor job ratings is one of the hardest things she has had to do. But in order to get some of her staff to do their work properly (so that the children get their dental care) she takes the heat. Many times she has done work (such as writing grants, requesting funding at counsel meetings, or giving presentations) that a person in a higher position might have been expected to do. Recently, Dr. S. Hubbard helped obtain funds to get a fully equipped mobile dental office for her region. When no one else would agree to drive this very large van, she stepped up to the plate. It required her to have training and take a test for a commercial trucker's license. There she was, a petite dentist and then regional director spending hours (much of her own time) learning to drive a large truck. Both the thought of driving this huge vehicle and taking a trucker's test were not pleasing to her, but she was willing to try (for the sake of the children and her program). Needless to say, the day she drove that big rig up to the office, with trucker's license in hand, there was much laughter and cheers (as well as silent thanks from people secretly glad not to be behind the wheel). And guess what? Because of her attitude to do whatever needs to be done (i.e., not merely her job description), Dr. Suzanne Hubbard has always been rapidly promoted; recently, she reached the top of her field as the Director of an entire state dental health program. The most amazing thing of all is that Suzanne demonstrated this level of responsibility at work while always putting her family first. She always supported her husband's work, and often made sacrifices to help him. If her children needed to see a doctor, be taken to a friend's home, go to dance class, or one of a million other things, she was there for them to the best of her ability. (Thanks, Sue! You are an exceptional wife and role-model for our children).

Take responsibility at **home.** When you and your spouse have a problem, take responsibility for trying to solve it and restoring harmony. Admit to your mistakes, shortcomings, and poor behavior. This will help you find the solutions to your conflicts because it is easier to change yourself than trying to change your spouse. You will be surprised how forgiving your wife or husband can be when they see you take responsibility instead of making excuses or hurling accusations at them. Put yourself in the hot seat and they won't need to put you there.

Try not to excessively blame your spouse when times are tough. Let's face it, tough times befall every couple. As we tell some of our clients who blame everything on their spouse, "You may be right, but you can be right all the way to divorce court." A common area of stress for married couples of all ages is financial stress. Do you find yourself getting a new credit card to pay off an old one? Or have you ever put your phone on voicemail to keep from talking to bill collectors? Debt is a very common problem in the U.S. Instead of using your energy arguing with each other, try to use that same energy to resolve your money problems together. For example, it may be vital that you sit down together and pay the bills, so that both of you see where you stand financially each month. Then together, use your imagination to find ways to save money and to increase your income. Married couples need to take responsiblility for this area, both as individuals, and as a couple.

Many times a wife or husband just needs to know that you realize there is a problem and are willing to work on it with them. Often they just need your attention, support, and understanding. Really listen to your spouse and absorb what she or he is saying. Here is a special message to men: It is okay to say, "Honey, you are right." Too often men assume they have the high ground and are reluctant to say they are sorry. The bigger you are the easier it is to say, "I was wrong. I will do better next time." And ladies, be sure to do the same when appropriate. Be a blessing to your spouse and they will be a greater blessing to you.

If you have **children**, be aware of the great responsibility you have as a parent. Children are by definition not totally responsible for themselves. You and your spouse should visualize the same basic expectations for your children. Try to give your children clear and consistent messages about what the two of you expect. Parents are much more effective (especially with difficult children) when they get on the same page with expectations and enforce them equally. Letting your child put you and your spouse on opposite sides of an issue can be bad for him or her as well as for the two of you. Discuss disputes in private, then present a united front. Help teach your children to take ever-increasing responsibility for their actions. Teach them right from wrong by example. That is one of the most important lessons you will ever impart.

Most importantly, take responsibility for your own **happiness**. Your feelings are your feelings. Take responsibility for them. What do "victimized" people say? "She made me mad." "My son made me angry." "My wife depresses me." Don't blame your parents, children, spouse, or boss for your unhappiness. Being happy is up to you. Happiness is an ATTITUDE that you develop or you neglect. Try not to blame your income, job, race, gender, or stresses. Sadly, many people do. Happiness is more a state of mind than a set of circumstance. By not blaming your parents, you can grow to be a mature and emotionally healthy adult. By not blaming your wife or husband, you won't have so many arguments or reasons for resentment. By not blaming your boss, you can stay focused and become more effective at work. There is a spiritual song that says, "It's not my brother, it's not my sister, but it's me oh, Lord, standing in the need of prayer."

In all things, do what is right if you want to find true happiness. If you find yourself hiding your behaviors, being embarrassed by what you do, rationalizing your actions, or continually looking over your shoulder to see who is watching, then you probably need to re-think what you are doing. Your heart will tell you what is right and wrong.

Life can be difficult. To be alive is to have stress. However, it is not stress that makes you unhappy; it is how you *react* to your stress. If you name a thousand reasons to be sad, what good will that do? But if you name one reason to be happy, what good will that do! Be thankful. Happiness is a STATE OF MIND, not a state of perfect conditions.

There is an often-told story about a man named Bill that goes something like this:

Bill came to work one day with his lunch box in his hand. At lunchtime he sat down, opened up his lunch pail and said, "What a bummer. Peanut butter and jelly sandwiches for twelve straight days!"

A guy sitting next to him looked at him and said, "Man, why don't you talk to your wife and have her put something else in there?"

Bill replied, "I'm not married. I made the sandwiches myself."

A lot of bad situations in life are the peanut butter and jelly sandwiches that we make. Once you start accepting this, you will start to grow and become more content. Understand that your situation is largely of your own making and your future will depend more on your ATTITUDE than almost anything else. Your emotional response to your problems is YOUR CHOICE. Take responsibility and set yourself free.

* * * *

TRY THESE IDEAS:

1. Write down the three most common excuses you make. Decide today that you will take responsibility in each of these areas.

2. Watch the excuses other people make. See if their excuses help their image, their character, or their relationships.

3. Take responsibility for a problem at home or work and watch how it affects the way others think of you.

* * * *

Suggested Affirmation: Say at least 10 times out loud, "I feel freer and lighter because I take responsibility for my life."

* * * *

Write down the most important thing(s) to remember from this Pearl:

_____

_____

_____

_____

PEARL # 2

———— ⚬⚬ ————

Quietly Reflect on Your Life

"A life not reflected upon is a life not worth living."
—Plato

"Self-knowledge is the beginning of self-improvement."
—Spanish proverb

"Most people search high and wide for the key to success. If they only knew the key to their dreams lies within."
—George Washington Carver

* * * *

"I'm late, I'm late for a very important date. No time to say hello, goodbye, I'm late, I'm late," exclaimed the White Rabbit in *Alice in Wonderland*. Does this sound like you? Many people today live fast-paced, hectic lives. However, it has been said that the busier you are, the more you need to take time to slow down and reflect. We emphasize the importance of self-reflection early in this book because it is so important (and difficult).

As you work through this book, try to schedule time to quietly reflect on your life. Reflect on where your life has been, where you are, where you are going, and where you need to go. Reflection helps you understand the journey you are on. Sometimes the direction you "want" to go and the direction you "need" to go are not the same. Ask yourself what is the right direction to go? Pray about it and search your heart. The lack of self-reflection is a major deficit in many people's lives. Why? Because it is hard work and people's lives are often too cluttered with less important activities (such as watching television or playing computer games). Honest self-assessment is mentally taxing and requires self-discipline to make any needed improvements.

In his leadership series, best selling author and management consultant John Maxwell refers to reflections as "taking time to develop the leader within us." Susan Taylor, in her book *Lessons in Living*, calls it "taking quiet time for yourself and asking yourself, How am I doing?" Stephen Covey calls it taking time to "sharpen your saw." Jim Rohn, America's foremost business philosopher and motivational speaker, calls it "taking time in sober reflection." Archbishop and Nobel Prize winner, Desmond Tutu says, "One spends a lot of time talking but not enough time listening." Deepak Chopra calls reflection "meditation and going deep inside yourself." *The Bible (Psalm 46:10)* says to "Be still and know."

Have you ever heard people say, "I got my best ideas on vacation or alone in the shower"? Others get inspiration while sitting on the toilet stool or in the middle of the night when they can't sleep. Dr. Hubbard, as a scientist, always got his most creative research ideas when he was taking a long drive in his car. For him, working in the biochemistry laboratory was merely putting into action those creative ideas that came to him away from the workplace. By quieting yourself in reflection, you will notice improved energy levels and expansion of your creativity. The process itself will relax you.

You will hear your inner conscience telling you what you need, what is right and how to solve your problems.

We suggest that you reflect on *positive* things in your life first. How can a person improve his or her self-esteem, mood, and happiness if he or she dwells on the negatives? For those of you who insist on starting with negative reflections, that is better than nothing. Start somewhere, anywhere, but get started reflecting on your life. But again, we suggest you start with positive reflections. A thankful heart heals many wounds. Think about your family, the things you are most proud of, and all of your other blessings. Put a smile on your face when you do this and notice your energy level exploding and glowing. Of these, think most about your loved ones. Think of the good times you have had with your spouse (if you're married) and children. *Reflect on those times of family fun and family laughter.* Notice how the laughter is surfacing in your heart as your reflect on this. Think of special holiday times and vacations. Remember the hugs and kisses on cold winter nights. Recall the victories you have had together. When all is said and done, you will not wish that you spent more time watching TV sit-coms or putting in more overtime at work. You will think about the time you shared with your loved ones.

Treat your loved ones like the special people they are and show appreciation to them as often as you can. Then start noticing how they respond to you in return. Too often people do just the opposite. People often take their loved ones for granted and even make them the targets of their frustrations. Has your spouse ever acted angry toward

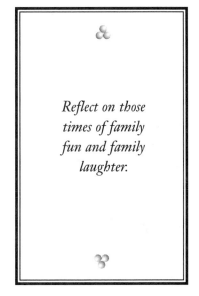

Reflect on those times of family fun and family laughter.

you, when he or she was really upset with someone at work? Has your spouse ever dumped on you, when it was really the kids (or themselves) he or she was mad at? This way of treating the ones you love isn't right or healthy, is it? Remember how valuable your family is to you and they will value you all the more. Why don't you pick up the phone right now and tell your spouse, child, or parent "I love you"?

Think for a moment about your *friends*. Do your friends know how much you appreciate them? Are the people you hang out with good for you? Are you a good influence on them? Many people called "friends" are just temporary acquaintances (not that we discourage these relationships), or may be using you for one purpose or another. True friends care for you in good times and bad. They encourage you and desire the best for you and your family. They are not selfish or self-centered. They rejoice in your achievements rather than become jealous of them. They empathize with you in your sorrow and try to make things better if they can. True friends are hard to find and are truly valuable. Many people may know only one or two such friendships in a lifetime. Try not to neglect them. So stay in touch with them as often as possible even though they may live far away. Let them know you value them enough to make a phone call.

Also reflect on how you treat other people around you. How you treat people who have little to give back to you is perhaps one of the greatest measures of your character. Being kind to your boss is one thing, but being nice to a junior coworker or subordinate is another. Holding a door open for a beautiful lady reflects less on man's character than holding the same door for an elderly woman. Show kindness to people and your reward will be much greater than theirs. As one bumper sticker says, "Jesus is coming. Quick, look like you are doing something."

Reflect on your *education*. Has your education stopped? Are you getting smarter or are you losing ground? Do you need to complete your formal education? Education improves your attitude and how you approach life. Formal education provides valuable credentials and is a solid path to success. But education also comes from the books you read, the tapes you listen to, and the people you are around. Earl Nightgale said, "If you study just one hour per day in your chosen profession, in three years you will be a national expert." Try to carry a pen and note pad with you in order to write down great ideas as you get them throughout the day. You may then want to record your ideas in a journal. A journal of ideas may be just what you need to get you headed toward some great opportunities. How many times did you wish you had captured a great idea but it slipped away because you didn't have a pen or paper to write it down? How many times did you go to bed and dream about a good idea, only to wake up and wish you had a pen and paper on your nightstand to capture that thought? Audiotapes, books, CD's, seminars, church, colleagues, friends, mentors, family—these and many other places are sources of great ideas. Consider where your education needs are. It is never too late!

Reflect on new approaches you can make to improve your education. Do you need to get your G.E.D., take a college course, or attend a seminar? Do you need to read or listen to audiotapes more? By becoming an audiotape listener, you transform your car into a "university on wheels" as Brian Tracy often tells his audiences. Knowledge and education expand your mind, give you new skills, increase your credentials, and lead you to new opportunities. To enjoy excellence, you have to enjoy learning.

Your mom and dad probably taught you far more than you could ever imagine. Sometimes parents set good examples, and sometimes not. So parents, think about what you are teaching your children through your words and behavior. Are you teaching them good habits, faith, and self-esteem? Are you being a good role model? Children do what you do, not what you say. You can tell them not to smoke, but if you smoke, guess what they're likely to do? Children are skilled copycats.

Think about your *accomplishments* and *leadership roles*. What have you already accomplished in your life? We bet you have accomplished more than you think. Did you help your workplace accomplish their goals? Did you give birth to a child? Did you help to raise a child? Did you help put a child through school? Do you lead a cub scout or girl scout group? Did you donate your time or money to your church? Not everyone is meant to win a Nobel Prize or be the MVP in a World Series. We all have small and large accomplishments. The funny thing is that you may not know which accomplishment was big and which one was small! Which is the more *important* achievement: being the MVP of a World Series or beating alcoholism? The MVP award is a fantastic honor, but does it have any real impact on the world? Achieving sobriety, on the other hand, can save your marriage and make you a better parent. To be an astronaut is a great accomplishment. But does it beat giving life, worth, or faith to a child? Does it beat creating a loving home for your family? Count all your accomplishments and be thankful for the opportunities you have had. As a motivational speaker, Earl keeps a testimonial reflection sheet on himself with positive statements others have said about his speaking presentations. Everyone needs encouragement, including you.

Have you accomplished things through other people? Perhaps you have made a real difference in the life of your children, spouse, or close friend. "There is leader within all of us," said Noel Thichy in his book *Leadership Engine*. In his seminars he asks attendees to review their lives and think about the leadership success they have enjoyed over the years. What event (in sports, church, school, family, etc.) would never have occurred successfully if you had not led the way? Take a few minutes and think about that. Write it down. Did it involve your child, a student, coworker, or spouse? Thichy feels this exercise helps people reflect on their leadership potential; it becomes a great energizer and confidence builder. So, reflect on your accomplishments and how your leadership led to the accomplishments of others.

Also think about the areas of your life that you need to *improve*. Everyone can improve. It is no disgrace. In what ways would you like to become more successful? Where do you need to change your attitude? Would you like to be a better parent, wealthier, leaner, healthier, or better educated? Do you need more balance in your life? Do you need to give more of your time to your spouse or your children? Do you need more enthusiasm at work? Do you need to curb your anger or your appetite? Reflect on these questions. But when you do, remember this **WARNING**—Don't be too hard on yourself! Guilt can be a very destructive emotion; when overemphasized, it simply won't help you. Most people are already their own worse critics. Whipping yourself over and over again for past "mistakes" or perceived weaknesses has no useful purpose! Rather, reflect on your past mistakes, ask for forgiveness, and learn from them. Who knows, some things you call "mistakes" today may turn out to be the "right" thing in the long run. It happens more than you think. For example, a job change may seem disastrous now, but prove to be a blessing later. It happens to many people. You don't have to look far to find them. Reflect on your weakness and deficiencies and let them inspire you to grow. Be honest with yourself, but also be generous with yourself. Who does not have weaknesses? If YOU can't be nice to YOU, then who will be?

Finally, reflect on *special mentors* who have had a positive influence on your life. They might be your parents, children, spouse, friends, teachers, coaches, or grandparents. What did they teach you? Do you need to be reminded of those lessons now? Perhaps these people built up your self-esteem, made connections for you, or passed on some of their experience and wisdom to you. Can you do the same for someone else? Reflect on the people you admire

most. How can you be more like them? What was the most important message they taught you? Write it down NOW and reflect on
how you are applying it in your life. Are you passing this message
on to others? You need mentors, but you should also be mentoring
others. You have more to teach than you realize. Try not to sell
yourself short. If you are reading this book, then you can teach others to read.

Find a special time and a special place for reflection. Some people like to go on long walks or take a drive to think. Other people
may like to sit under a tree, by a lake, or on a hill. Still others may
have a cozy place at home next to the fire to reflect. Make it a time
and place that helps you relax, concentrate, and think. It may also
be a good time to pray. Make it a place you enjoy.

Some of you may say, "I don't have any time to think! I have too
many children. I have too many work hours. I have too many things
to do." Wrong! If you are that over-burdened, that overwhelmed,
then you must take time to reflect. Not reflecting on what you are
doing and how you are prioritizing your time may be why you are
overwhelmed. Of the many things you do each day, few things will
be as important as taking time to reflect. People make time for the
things they need to do.

One good way to reflect on yourself is through the eyes of others. See your reflection in the eyes of your children, husband or
wife, workmates and friends. What do they think about you? Does
your workplace see you as a special asset? If not, why not? Do your
children want to be like you when they grow up? Does your wife or
husband think they are blessed to have you as their spouse? Viewing
yourself through the eyes of others can be enlightening. Take time
to reflect, pray, and plan. Life is a precious gift and you have to
reflect on your life to celebrate this great blessing.

* * * *

TRY THESE IDEAS:

1. Mark on your calendar important birthdays, anniversaries, and other dates that show people you care about them.

2. Tell your spouse (or loved one) how special he or she is to you. Pick up the phone and do it NOW or you may forget to do it. Husbands and wives are very special people and need to be told so.

3. Reflect on the values that you are teaching your children. Are you a good role model? How can you be a better example for them?

4. Where and when do you take the time to reflect on your life? Do you have a special place to think? Be sure to find a special place to think, relax, pray, and reflect.

* * * *

Suggested Affirmation: Say to yourself 10 times out loud, "I am taking responsibility to reflect on my life. This reflection time is helping me to enhance my happiness."

* * * *

Write down the most important thing(s) to remember from this Pearl:

_____

_____

_____

_____

PEARL # 3

Do It With Passion

"What counts is not necessarily the size of the dog in the fight, but the size of the fight in the dog."
—Dwight D. Eisenhower

"Nothing great was ever achieved without enthusiasm."
—Ralph Waldo Emerson

"The secret of happiness is not in doing what you like, but in liking what you are doing."
—Sir James M. Barrie

* * * *

CAROL HYATT, a seasoned presenter with the National Association of Female Executives (NAFE) delivered a keynote address to NAFE members years ago and spoke about how they could find their passion in life. She instructed the audience to identify their primary job title and quickly write three of their top duties. After they completed this task, she told them to circle the one they enjoyed the most. That became their "A passion" area. Then she then asked them to write down their favorite hobby. The audience did so. She told them that their hobby was their "B passion." Finally, Ms. Hyatt asked each audience member to combine "A passion" and "B passion" in some way and to imagine (or visualize) what their passion in life might be. Take time and try this exercise yourself.

What discoveries did you make? Were you able to combine your favorite job duty with your hobby to find your passion? Earl did this exercise during one of her seminars. At the time, he was director of an outpatient hospital at Ridgeview Institute in Atlanta, and his top duties were as follows: 1) supervising his staff; 2) making presentations to outside companies and organizations as well as lecturing to patients in his program; 3) writing policies and procedures for the agency manual. His hobbies were playing sports (such as tennis) and watching basketball. Earl enjoyed his number two duty of making presentations and his hobby was sports. He is now an international motivational speaker and consultant to the NBA (National Basketball Association) and the NFL (National Football League). Earl has been able to combine his favorite job duty with his favorite hobby to realize his dream. Give it some thought. Loving your job makes a huge difference. As the saying goes, "people who love their jobs never have to work."

> *One of the obvious differences between successful people and those who merely survive is their level of passion for the things they do.*

One of the obvious differences between successful people and those who merely survive is their level of passion for the things they do. As Dale Carngie has said, "You never achieve real success unless you like what you are doing." Passion is getting fired up! Passion is the great energizer and motivator. Passion brings spice to your life. Passion not only feels good to you, but also to those around you. If you have great enthusiasm for your faith, marriage, family, and work, you are bound to be happy and successful. The passion we refer to is of course that which makes you a better person, not inappropriate passion. You know the difference. Inappropriate passion (such as selfish behaviors, recklessness, affairs, and others) destroys, while the type of passion we are discussing builds.

You will radiate energy when you develop greater passion. In fact, as a living creature you are already literally an energy machine. Your body turns food into energy every moment of every day. Passion gives you more energy. It stokes the fire. Watch a person who has great passion for his or her job and you will find someone who rarely watches the clock—in fact, he or she may need to be reminded that it is time to go home. Turn up the heat for the things you do at work and at home.

Have you ever had an outstanding coach or teacher? What made them different from the others? In most cases it wasn't so much what they knew, but the joy and passion they had for what they were doing. Dr. Hubbard went to a crippled children's school in the third grade (on crutches or in a wheelchair) for a disease that affected his legs. He did not know if he would ever walk again. Although he cannot recall his teacher's name now, Dr. Hubbard will never forget the love his 3rd grade teacher had for teaching handicapped children and the tears on her face when, near the end of that year, he walked into the classroom, healed.

Doesn't it feel good to be around people who have passion for what they are doing? When you are excited, people want to be around you because you generate passion inside them! Life can be hard; so people are always seeking out energy and passion. People want to be energized by it and filled with it. When they see passion in someone else it becomes contagious. They want to be around that person. Great politicians, athletes, and religious leaders generate passion in their fans or followers. In his book, *Principle-Centered Leadership*, Stephen Covey says that an effective leader should "radiate positive energy." So ask yourself, "What kind of energy do I radiate every day?" Are you radiating positive energy at home, at work, and with friends? It has been said enthusiasm is the number one leadership quality.

Find out where your passions lie so that you can actively cultivate them. Develop greater enthusiasm at home and at work. Do you have a passion for taking care of children, business, medical care, teaching, sports, money, art, or something else? Passion is the fuel that will help make your dreams come true. An excellent illustration of enhancing your life with passion is from the movie "City Slickers." In the film the main character is bored and unhappy at work (selling radio airtime). He experiences a great deal of excitement, anxiety, and adventure as a "dude" on a cowboy ranch, only to realize that his passion is back at home with his family. He came to understand that, because it helped his family, his work was actually a great blessing and something about which he could be excited. He realized that to enjoy life, he did not have to change his work; he only needed to "do it better." That is, to do it with more passion. He decided to strive for excellence. Previously his lack of passion at work spilled over at home. So he had to change his attitude at work to fully enjoy his home. Although this is only a movie, it illustrates what happens to many people who do not have passion for what they do at work or at home. Some people require major changes in their lives, but most need only a change of their attitudes and habits. Passion is an attitude that you can amplify if you need to.

You don't have to be a rocket scientist or an astronaut to have fun and passion for what you do. You can generate fun and create passion wherever you are. Even if you have a tough job that you can't change for financial reasons, you may find more passion by the way you interact with your coworkers. A mother can feel totally overwhelmed taking care of her children or make it the most fulfilling job on earth. Another great image to have from the movies is that of Maria in the "The Sound of Music." Her joyful passion for taking care of a widower's children was so great that it was infectious. Even the sad widower learned to sing, laugh, and be happy again. He too began to interact more with his children in a loving fashion. Everyone enjoyed Maria's company because of the zest she had for life.

Have passion for the LITTLE things in life. This is important because the little things far outnumber the big things! Be like the 4- or 5-year-old who charges out of bed each morning, anticipating a day of fun and excitement. That same child hates to go to bed at night because there are so many things left to do. Are you like this little child? Sometimes becoming a successful adult means you have to take on some of the behaviors of little children. Enjoy the little things your children do and show enthusiasm for the things they enjoy. For example, play hide-and-seek with the enthusiasm of your children, and your children will remember it forever.

For those of you who are married, bring renewed passion to your marriage. Get excited about a special meal that was prepared for you by your spouse. Be happy about the paycheck your spouse brings home each month. He or she worked very hard for that money. Try not to take things for granted. Try not to ask yourself *if* you still feel passion for your wife or husband, but rather, *how* to show it. The more you show it, the more it will grow. Most people follow their feelings. That is, their actions follow their feelings. For many occasions that is fine. But the opposite is also true. That is, *feelings will follow actions*. If you don't treat your wife or husband special, you won't think of them as special. *You* will reap great rewards when your actions make your spouse feel special. Wives need to be told how wonderful and beautiful they are by their husbands. And husbands need to be told how important and handsome they are to their wives. You owe it to your wife or husband to keep the kisses flowing and the hugs warm. Go out on dates and special getaways no matter how many years you have been married. Go to the movies, go dancing, or just find a quite place together. Walking together at night or in the morning is a great way to bond. Keep in touch and communicate often. Your spouse is sharing his or her life with you. What greater gift could anyone give you? Not only will you and your wife or husband benefit from the greater love in your relationship, but your children will surely benefit, too.

Here are two warnings: First, try not to harm your relationship with your spouse or children by letting the passion for your job consume you. Balance is extremely important. Passion for your work should not translate into neglect of your family. Some people have jobs such as sales, military service, consultant services, and other occupations that take them away for periods of time. If you can't be home every night, make sure your family knows that you want to be with them. Call as often as possible. Make sure they know you love them.

Second, don't let the love and passion for your children interfere with the love and passion for your wife or husband. Children have to come first much of the time, but *not* all of the time. Mutual love between parents is a great gift to their children. Let the love and care for your spouse be readily apparent to your children. By doing so, you'll provide them an invaluable model for a loving, happy family.

* * * *

TRY THESE IDEAS:

1. Generate passion and energy at work. Observe how it makes you and other people feel.

2. Be passionate about what your children are doing. Enjoy activities with them often.

3. Go on a date with your wife or husband at least once a week. Let your spouse know you care and that you consider yourself blessed to be married to him or her.

* * * *

Suggested Affirmations: Say out loud 10 times, "I am pursuing and creating my passions at home and work. It is refueling me to become stronger and more successful than ever before."

* * * *

Write down the most important thing(s) to remember from this Pearl:

_____

_____

_____

_____

Congratulations! You made it past three Pearls. This puts you ahead of most other people. Keep going if you want to keep growing. Good luck.

PEARL # 4

&

Be Thankful

"Start where you are and with what you have,
knowing that what you have is plenty enough."
—Booker T. Washington

"When God wants to send us a gift, he tends to
send it in a form of a problem."
—W. Clement Stone

"Let the peace of Christ rule in your hearts…
And be thankful."
—Paul, Colossians 3:15, Bible

* * * *

ISN'T IT A PLEASURE to be around someone with a thankful heart? Not long ago, Dr. Hubbard met an eighty-year-old volunteer at a nearby hospital. She was always full of good cheer and thankfulness. Usually Dr. Hubbard was too busy to speak at length with her, but one day he had the time to chat a little longer. To his surprise, Dr. Hubbard found out that this happy and active person was actually under a great deal of stress. Her husband, whom she loved very much, had cancer and was not doing well. The numerous operations to remove the cancer had left him disfigured and discouraged. She also had a few of her own medical problems, as you might expect of a person her age. Despite all of this, she still volunteered at the hospital and joyfully helped others in need. She said that she felt very thankful to the Lord for her blessings and wanted to give something back. What a lesson she teaches us about the power of faith and gratitude. (Note: Just prior to the completion of this book her husband died. She is still volunteering at the hospital and still has a thankful heart. God bless her.)

Life is full of paradoxes and there is a particularly important paradox that you need to keep in mind while reading this book. *You should strive to be better, but you must also be very thankful for what you have now.* So while you work to grow and improve, also be content and thankful for what you have now and what you have already accomplished. This balance in thinking will help you to be happy now and help you move forward as well. Being thankful now is very important because there are so many forces in our world that foster discouragement, derailment, and discontent. For example, watch how many advertising commercials make you feel that you don't have a cool enough car, a pretty enough dress, the right figure, or enough minutes on your cell phone. Again, this is a book about self-improvement, but it is also a book to encourage peace and contentment within your own heart. Write down the things you have to be thankful for. We suggest that you do it now. We bet that once you get going, the list will grow larger than you ever imagined. Keep that list nearby and refer to it often.

> *You should strive to be better, but you must also be very thankful for what you have now.*

Begin by being thankful to your parents, grandparents, godparents, or foster parents (whoever it was that raised you). Your parents gave you life and hopefully love. Loving mothers are particularly special people. They carry babies inside their bodies for months despite discomfort and concerns about their figure. After that they face painful and possibly even life-threatening labor. Then they devote the next twenty years of their life to helping that child become a good and happy adult. Truly loving mothers are one of God's greatest gifts.

If you have (or had) loving parents, then you have a great deal to be thankful for! Starting out in life with caring parents is a huge advantage in this world. It sets your feet solidly underneath you because the feeling of love is so important to the human spirit. Good parents (or loving caretakers) give so much and ask for so little back. Parents are "on call 24-7" and give up many aspects of their own lives to better their children's lives. Thank your parents many times and in many ways. Usually it is your love and attention that is their favorite gift.

The incredible gift of your parents can only be fully appreciated when you are a parent, too. Few things will change your life more than your first baby. No job will be more demanding than parenthood. So leave this Pearl for a moment and call up your parents and say "I'm thankful for all you did for me. I love you." They will be thrilled to hear from you, and more importantly they will receive your appreciation with excitement. If one or both have passed away, say a prayer for them and openly express to God your gratitude for them.

What about those people who truly did not have loving parents? We know that some people have major issues with their parents. Maybe one of your parents had a drug or alcohol problem. Maybe your dad had a temper or your mother was depressed. In these cases it is important to try and find forgiveness in your heart, even if you think they don't deserve it. For your sake, and theirs, try to find forgiveness. They too are (or were) only human. They too may have grown up under horrible circumstances. Perhaps they were struggling month to month just to make it financially, but you were too young or busy to notice. Maybe they were abused as a child. These are not things that excuse poor treatment of any child, but may help you understand a little better and forgive a little easier.

For some people, professional help may be needed to treat chronic depression, anxiety, anger, fear, substance abuse, and other possible consequences of a problematic childhood. For others, perhaps a grandparent, aunt, or godparent intervened and provided support during your childhood. If so, they deserve a huge thanks from you. Be thankful to whoever helped you in your formative years and don't let regrets or resentments from those years hold you back now!

Parents be thankful for your *children*. What beautiful blessings they are. Children will take more time, effort, and energy out of you than any job. And yet, the effort you put into them somehow becomes proportional to how much you come to love them. When you see your children playing quietly together, stop and give them praise. Many times, we only give them attention when they are misbehaving. Start teaching them affirmations early in life. Your primary job is to love them, teach them, protect them, build their self-esteem, and encourage their spiritual growth. Most of the things parents get mad about with their children are just normal childhood behaviors. Try laughing more with them than scolding them. Love a child and they will love you back. There is no greater gift than love. Be thankful for your children. They grow up, but they will always be yours. Children bring meaning and happiness to life. When was the last time you really hugged your children? Remember to give them (including your young sons) a hug the next time you see them. Be sure to pray in thanksgiving for your children.

Be thankful for your *spouse*. A loving wife or husband is one of the most wonderful blessings in the world. Your husband or wife shares their life with you. What an amazing gift that is! They struggle with you during hard times and laugh with you during good times. Help to build each other's self-esteem and be determined to be a blessing to each other. You will be the winner as well as your spouse. Try to give your marriage the special reverence it deserves. Remember, marriages are generally conducted by ministers (or priests) because they are religious ceremonies, not just a social promise. Every marriage has its ups and downs. In part, that is because life and people have their ups and downs. Do not be surprised by troubles; but be determined to resolve them. In hard times remind yourself about the things that attracted you to your wife or husband. Perseverance, love, and faith are vital. So is sharing. Doesn't a beautiful day mean more when shared with a loving wife or husband? Isn't it nice to live with someone who shares the same memories? Let your wife or husband know how thankful you are for them.

Married couples need to spend time ALONE together away from the children. Too often couple's time is a neglected area after children come along. Parenting is very hard, time-consuming work. Grandparents and other relatives should help couples by baby-sitting the children as much as possible. Most children love their grandparents and don't mind time away from their parents now and then. Let the grandparents spoil your children while you and your spouse spoil each other.

Be thankful for your *work*. People need work. It helps give purpose and direction to life. Your work may be as a mother, business owner, laborer, or corporate executive. It makes little difference what you do, if you are thankful for it. Everyone who does honest work should be proud of his or her work. Being proud of what you do is important to your self-esteem. Try not to let the media fool you to believe that athletes, models, movie stars, or other celebrities are the only ones who should be proud of their jobs. The truth is, these "famous" people are mostly just entertainers who owe their fame and wealth to promoters and mass media technology. Before radio, movies, television, and CDs came along, even very talented entertainers could barely make a living as traveling performers. The fact is, society needs a lot of different people doing a lot of different things. Teachers, preachers, clerks, fireman, doctors, nurses, business people, lawyers, typists, line workers, soldiers, motivational speakers, and many others all serve vital roles. Find the niche that suits your talents and you will be happier. As they say, a person who enjoys his job never has to work for a living.

Be thankful to live in *America*. Life can be hard. Taxes, bosses, traffic jams, bills, and many other stressors make it hard to remember to be thankful. But think about it for a moment. And say to yourself out loud, "I am living in the best country in the world and that's why so many people want to come here." Americans are greatly blessed. Thank a veteran sometime. They helped to preserve your liberty. Perhaps that veteran is your dad or your grandfather. America is the land of opportunity and freedom. You can find almost any type of climate here from the cold of Vermont to the Florida sun. It is a country powerful enough to protect itself and strong enough to help its friends. Do you know a country where a poor person can own their own business, become wealthy, or go into politics so easily? Do you know a country where the main obstacle to success is your own lack of effort? Many of the people we call "poor" in America would be considered extremely fortunate in many parts of the globe. America has land, freedom, easy access to education, jobs of all types, laws to protect, and no rival in military defense. Be thankful for living in the U.S.A.

Be thankful for the *little things* that make you happy. This is so important because the little things are what make up most of our lives! Be thankful for the smell of the air in spring, the warmth of a fire in winter, the crisp air in the fall, and the feel of the ocean breeze in summer. If you don't have four seasons where you live it must be that you love the warm climate of a place like Southern California or the unique beauty of a land like Alaska. Be thankful for the child's hand you hold or the affectionate hug from your husband or wife. Enjoy the birds when they sing and the softness of a baby's cheek when you give one a kiss. Be thankful that you are safe and not in harm's way. Some soldiers may be facing war this very day. Be thankful you are not hungry but have food on your plate. Be thankful for all these things and more because thankfulness allows you to enjoy them more fully. People who are grateful for the "little things" in life are happy people.

Finally, thank *God* for everything! God wants to help you out of your problems, if you let Him in through prayer and faith. The Bible says that all truly good things in your life are blessings from God. Your Heavenly Father wants the best for you and you should want to be your best for God. The Bible teaches that God does not create the problems on Earth. Instead, problems arise as a result of our sins and our distance from Him.

As a child, Dr. Hubbard heard a preacher tell a story about a boy who did not have a loving father. In fact, the father had been the town drunk before being shipped off to jail. The preacher knew of the boy's troubling situation and felt compassion for him. As the boy left church one day, the two shook hands as the preacher said, "You know, I know your father." The boy looked up, suddenly ashamed (not that a child should bear blame for a parent), and unsure of what to say. The preacher continued. "Yes, I know your father. He watches out for you every day. You see, he is my Father, too." The boy was confused and surprised for a moment, but then understood. We all have the same Father.

Isn't it nice to know that you are never alone or forsaken? As told by the prophet Isaiah, "So do not fear, for I am with you; do not be dismayed, for I am your God. I will strengthen you and help you;

I will uphold you with my righteous right hand" (Isaiah 41:10). Be thankful for your Heavenly Father who made you, loves you, and cares more about you than any person can. Whom else can you turn to when the world is collapsing around you? Whom else can you trust so much? Who else has so much power, wisdom, and authority? And who else would sacrifice their son for you so that you may have life, and have it more abundantly?

So approach today and every day with a sense of gratitude. Gratitude should come early and often. Give thanks in your thoughts, speech, and prayers. When you sincerely express thankfulness and gratitude, you open up the door to contentment, opportunity, and happiness.

* * * *

TRY THESE IDEAS:

1. Call your mom and dad to say "Thank you." Do it today.

2. Think about the USA and the vast opportunities we have compared to other nations.

3. Do something special for your wife or husband to let them know how much you are thankful for them.

4. Thank God for your life and all your blessings.

5. Go out and buy a bunch of "thank you" cards and start sending them out to deserving people.

* * * *

Suggested Affirmation: Say out loud 10 times, "I have much to be thankful for."

* * * *

Write down the most important thing(s) to remember from this Pearl:

_____

_____

_____

_____

PEARL # 5

Reprogram Your Mind With Positive Self-Talk

"The mind is ever the ruler of the universe."
—Plato

"The real voyage of discovery is not seeking new lands, but in seeing with new eyes."
—Marcel Proust

* * * *

YES, YOU CAN REPROGRAM YOUR MIND. Start this Pearl by saying to yourself out loud, "I believe they are right and I am reprogramming my mind with positive thoughts." By doing that, you have just started the programming process. Your brain is like a computer and you can be the programmer. The mind gathers information, processes it with millions of other pieces of information, and forms new conclusions every minute of every day. The human brain is simply the greatest wonder of the world! You are aware of part of this process (your conscious mind), but you are unaware of other parts of your mind's work (your unconscious and subconscious minds). In fact, most mental activity goes on without your being conscious of it. This helps prevent you from becoming overwhelmed with information, analysis, and future possibilities. Thoughts are made conscious on a "need to know" basis. For example, your breathing is usually regulated without your conscious effort even though you can control it. That is because you don't want to be thinking about how to take each breath.

How is your mind programmed, and by whom? This is an important question, isn't it? You get information and feedback, desired or not, from all sorts of people, places, and circumstances every day. And do you know what? Much of the programming and feedback you get is not good! The TV, newspapers and radio news is more often bad than good. Our society tends to focus more on what's wrong with people than on what's right. The world may tell you that you are too poor, old, fat, ugly, or a hundred other dreaded things. Many, if not most, people are not very interested in making you feel good about yourself. So ask yourself if the people you spend the most time with are truly good for you. Do they make you a better person?

We suggest that you become an audiotape listener of motivational tapes, so that you will hear frequent positive messages. Compare those messages to the messages sent to your brain by a lot of popular music and television these days. Their messages are often destructive to you and to society. They may seem harmless at first, but when put together with other harmful input from the world, they can create misleading impressions and negative programming in you and your children. Inappropriate sex, drug use, and violence are just a few of the areas that popular "entertainment" often promotes, either directly or indirectly. Children these days are bombarded with these messages because of the explosion of communications technology and the lack of safeguards. You, your spouse, and your children are not robots, but this sort of programming does influence people and can give people a warped sense of normality. So try to protect yourself and your family by searching for sources of positive messages.

Even people who love you may frequently tell you all the ways you are screwing up. Some husbands and wives do this to their spouse almost everyday. Unfortunately, much (or most) of your feedback is not confidence- building and confidence is the foundation for personal growth and self-esteem. In fact, the data going into your mind can be downright discouraging and destructive! So is it any surprise that many people suffer from high anxiety, depression, substance abuse, and/or low self-esteem? Start collecting books and motivational tapes that can help you stay positive in a world of too many negatives. See our bibliography for ideas.

Take control and responsibility to reverse the effect of some of the sarcasm, ridicule, and negative feedback that too often comes your way. Start by self-programming your mind with self-confidence and other important messages. *Remember, your mind does not control you. You must control your mind.* The problem is that most people are a slave to whatever direction their thoughts take them. You must take control of your thoughts. In the popular movie "The Matrix" people could program their minds in an instant by connecting their brain to a computer-like machine and putting in educational programs. In this movie one person learned martial arts in minutes and another learned to fly a helicopter in seconds. That would be nice wouldn't it? If you were in the matrix,

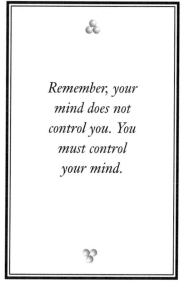

Remember, your mind does not control you. You must control your mind.

what program would you put in? How would you program your mind? How would you want to improve yourself? The fact is, you *can* program your mind in much the same way! Of course, life is not as Hollywood portrays it, so it will take more time, patience, and hard work. But it can be done. And look on the bright side, you won't need a metallic computer input port in the back of your head! You, too, can program your mind to learn karate, fly a helicopter, and be more self-confident. Others have done it. Why not you?

A proven way to expedite that process is regularly talking to yourself in such a way as to program your unconscious mind with the positive changes you want. Self-talk techniques, sometimes called "affirmations," have been studied for many years and determined to be successful.

Perhaps some of you are saying, "Talk to myself? That's ridiculous." But wait a moment. You already talk (or think) to yourself all the time don't you? And what do many people tell themselves? They think "I'm stupid," "I'm fat," "My boss hates me," "I'll never make anything of myself," or a million other negative thoughts. It's the truth, isn't it? What sort of negative programming have you been feeding your brain lately? Why let this important self-programming process be so negative and haphazard? Why not control, improve, and refine it? Why not replace society's anxiety- and fear-based programming with programming based on faith, growth, and self-confidence? Researchers say most self-talk is negative. If that is true, think about how all these negative thoughts have already affected your self-esteem, creativity, job performance, as well as your approach to your life. But just as negative thoughts can affect your life, so can positive ones!

Take the time to consciously reprogram your unconscious mind. Get your imagination going. You choose the programs. If you have problems with self-esteem, you may want to jump-start your brain by saying to yourself (about ten times a day), "I FEEL GOOD

ABOUT MYSELF" or "I FEEL FANTASTIC!" This is what Willie Jolly, noted motivational speaker, does with his audiences to start raising their self-esteem. This affirmation, said out loud, helps make your mind a servant to you by creating pictures you want to have. "Most people allow themselves to be a slave in their mind," said Glenna Salsburg, motivational speaker on personal development in her audiotape series called "Passion, Power and Purpose." If you are a sluggish person in the morning you may try saying out loud the next time you get up "I FEEL WIDE AWAKE" or "I'M THE BEST THING THAT EVER HAPPENED TO ME!" Then put a big smile on your face. In about five to ten minutes, you will notice a change in your attitude. Isn't it cool to think you can program your subconscious however you want? People are learning machines, more sophisticated than any computer. You are a learning machine. This aspect of humanity is one of the things that makes humans special above all other creatures on earth. It just takes practice and effort.

As discussed in Brian Tracy's audiobook, *The Psychology of Achievement*, affirmations are most effective when they employ the principle of the "three P's." Make your self-talk affirmations

(i) *personal* (i.e., use "I am" statements);

(ii) *positive* (such as "I am smart," rather than negative statements such as "I am not stupid"); and

(iii) *present tense* (such as "I am wealthy," rather than "I will be wealthy").

Of these three principles, the "present tense" component is often the hardest for many people to do. After all, at first it seems like a lie to say something like "I am a rich" instead of "I will be rich." It is not a lie. It is a technique to make you grow and achieve that goal. It is your right to be the programmer of your own mind. You do not owe an explanation to anyone else.

Some affirmations may even cause you to feel some initial tension because they are designed to challenge your old belief systems. That is fine. Eventually through practice and discipline your unconscious mind will resist less and less until it does not resist at all. It might be difficult to tell yourself "I am pretty" when you usually think you are not. But the fact is, that present tense is how the mind works. And remember, positive self-talk is merely a programming technique to help you grow and improve. It is a programming technique for your mind, not a false statement for others to hear. Other negative programs (such as the inappropriate comments of an ill-mannered date or coworker) may already be telling you that you are not pretty. They must be countered effectively. And by the way, beauty is not an absolute, it is subjective. As they say, it is in the eyes of the beholder. That is, it is all in the mind! So the more you program your mind towards a positive image of yourself, the easier it will be to accept. Self-talk statements must be in the "here and now" for your mind to change. If your subconscious thinks of you as rich, attractive, and confident NOW, then it will create the appropriate changes in your thought patterns, speech, body language, and even opportunities to support your new self-image! Remember, the mind is the most amazing and powerful object in the known universe! It can do wonderful things. However, it is up to you to make your mind function at its best.

Some of you may still think affirmations sound a little weird. But guess what? It works if you work at it. It works because this is how your mind already works. You are just trying to use the mind's natural processes to your greater advantage. Try lifting weights some time while telling yourself "I am weak... I am weak... I am weak." Then try it again as you tell yourself "I am strong ...I am strong...I am strong." What a difference a little reprogramming makes. Your mind is very powerful. What do you think effective coaches do when they talk to teams before a game? They try to program confidence into the minds of their players because they know the incredible difference it can make.

Many athletes use positive self-talk and programming. Athletes are not afraid to use something so simple, inexpensive, and powerful to give them a winning edge. Routinely used by doctors (and other healers) to help patients, positive affirmations are surely an important aspect of the "healing touch." But remember, positive self-talk is like anything else, the more you use it the more effective it will be. Don't think that saying a few positive self-talk statements a few times will change your life. That would be magic. This is not magic, but it is a powerful tool. You must repeat them frequently, perhaps ten to twelve times a day, until you begin to feel it is taking hold. Then, after progress has been made, you will need to jump-start the process now and then to prevent sliding back into old thought patterns. This technique is not meant to produce a conceited or phony you. It is a technique to make a better, calmer, and more effective you.

Keep in mind that you have been programmed since you were very young to be average or like everyone else. So start reprogramming yourself to become more than you have been. We suggest that you write your affirmations on 3 x 5 note cards or in a diary so that you read and repeat them everyday. Repeat the affirmations at least ten to twenty times a day for greatest results. Affirmations will increase your energy, your enthusiasm, and your passion.

The great thing about repeating affirmations is that you don't need a lot of time to work with them. You can say them while waiting in traffic, working at your job, in line at the store, picking up your children, out for a walk, in the bathtub, playing golf, or cooking a meal. But only choose two or three statements at one time. We've known people to list ten, twenty, and sometimes even thirty statements that they want to repeat to themselves everyday. You simply cannot work on so many things at once. Attempting to do so will water down your efforts because you won't be fully focused. Start with a short list. Perhaps use only two to five affirmations, but develop the habit of regularly working on them.

Affirmations will create a profound behavioral change in you when you regularly say them aloud or to yourself. Even if you are skeptical at the beginning, your affirmations somehow will begin acting on you faster than you thought. The more you internalize what you are saying to yourself on a daily basis, the more powerful it becomes. The more you repeat something, the more it becomes true. Your mind is simply a servant that obeys your orders.

So begin to utilize your inner power of positive self-talk. Bear in mind, it will take some practice, time, faith, and courage. It only works if you work at it. If you don't, it won't. Your words have a tremendous power. The Bible even describes Jesus as "the Word." So start saying those powerful words of affirmation over and over again and observe what happens to you. Say affirmations as you wake up each day. Say them before you go to an important meeting at work or say them before you make an important group presentation. Say them to help you become a better you.

* * * *

TRY THESE IDEAS:

1. Tell yourself "I am a calm and confident person" 5 to 10 times every morning and every night for two weeks and see how it feels.

2. Imagine what you would program into your mind if you could merely slip in a computer disc. What would you change about yourself at work? What would you change about yourself at home? What would you change about your self-image? Write these down on a 3x5 card and develop positive self-talk messages to program a better you.

* * * *

Suggested Affirmation: Say out loud 10 times, "I am programming my mind with good thoughts only."

* * * *

Write down the most important thing(s) to remember from this Pearl:

_____

_____

_____

_____

PEARL # 6

Reprogram Your Mind With Visualization

*"Man can only become what he is able to
consciously imagine."*
—Dane Rudhyar

*"Cherish your vision and your dreams
as they are the children of your soul;
the blueprints of your ultimate achievements."*
—Napoleon Hill

"Nothing happens unless first a dream."
—Carl Sandburg

"Imagination is more important than knowledge."
—Albert Einstein

* * * *

&

Visualizing your goals and dreams clearly in your mind is, therefore, another very important technique in programming your unconscious mind for success and excellence.

AS YOU BEGIN TO READ THIS PEARL, we want you to retrieve several magazines and newspapers to cut out pictures and articles of things that represent what you want to obtain or what you want to become in the next five years. For example, if you want to live in a four-bedroom home, find a picture in the real estate section of the newspaper that resembles the house you want. Or even better, go to model house openings in the type of neighborhood in which you want to live and collect pictures of houses that excite you. For example, Earl wanted to own a 7 Series BMW. To that end, he cut out a picture of a BMW as a reminder of his goal. He has also visited a BMW dealership for a testdrive and obtained a booklet of information about the car. And guess what. A year later he was driving a 7 Series BMW. Collect pictures of things you desire and paste them on a large piece of flip chart paper. Remember to paste the pictures on a large board and display it where you can see it every day. Dr. Hubbard has a picture of the next house he and his wife Suzanne plan to build displayed on his refrigerator. If it is a certain type of job that you desire cut out appropriate pictures that remind you of your goal. Some people refer to this technique as "treasure mapping." Now you are ready to read this Pearl because you are picturing what you want in life by using your brain power. As Marcus Aurelius said, "Our life is what our thoughts make it." Earl's wife Felicia Mabuza-Suttle (host of South Africa's top-rated talk-show`) says "Your mind is like a camera; it can take beautiful pictures that nourish your soul, or you can focus your lenses on ugly images that will destroy your mind."

To achieve something special, you need to have clear images of what you want to achieve. *Visualizing your goals and dreams clearly in your mind is, therefore, another very important technique in programming your unconscious mind for success and excellence.* For discussion, we will call the big, long-term hopes you have for the future your "dream" or "dreams." Your dream may be owning your own business, becoming a minister, making it in the NFL, graduating from college, being a wonderful mother, or perhaps becoming a millionaire. We will use the term "goals" to describe the smaller, well-defined things you want to accomplish. Examples of goals include getting a raise, passing a test, or losing ten pounds. Achieving your smaller goals will help make your dreams come true. Visualization of achieving both short-term goals and long-term dreams is both very important. One key to realizing your dreams is writing them down on paper in as much detail as possible. So start writing as you continue reading this Pearl.

To realize your dream(s) you must first have a dream. Martin Luther King had a dream for a racism-free America which led to his "I Have a Dream" speech. This speech is considered one of the most inspirational speeches of all time. Develop your goals and dreams in areas such as your career, health, marriage, education, friendships, and spiritual growth. Olympic athletes are outstanding examples of people who dream big and must constantly visualize their dream for many years before even getting a chance to compete at the Olympics. What faith they must have in their dreams.

What are your dreams? Do you know? Have you clearly envisioned a rewarding and exciting future? Do you want to own your own business, become a teacher, or be a wonderful mother and housewife? If money were no object, what would you do with your life? Get your imagination fired up! Would you change your work, move, paint, help children, or perhaps travel more? Who are you and why did God put you here? Perhaps you dream of being in the Peace Corps, going to medical school, being a fireman, or having children. Perhaps having more money is your dream. Do you dream of having enough money not to have to worry about money? That would be nice. It's your choice what to dream. Why sell yourself short? You only live once, so dream big! As they say, "Life is not a dress rehearsal." Children dream big. People need to learn from them. But remember this WARNING: We do not suggest that you dream at the expense of others, especially your family. Let them develop dreams with you. Remember the difference between worldly "success" and true "excellence" that we discussed in the preface. Excellence always embodies doing what is *right*; one can be selfish, wrong, or downright unethical, yet still meet the world's standards of success. *So be mindful **what** you dream, as well has **how** you pursue your dream.*

How can you start to achieve your dream? What goals will you have to accomplish along the way? Have you already started taking definitive steps to achieve your dreams? These questions are a good place to start. Visualizing your dream coming true and holding on to that vision are the two vital steps to realizing your dream. In a previous Pearl we talked about reprogramming your mind with self-talk. Visualization is also a form of reprogramming your mind. Use your imagination to its fullest. What visualization programs do you need to achieve your dreams? Do you need to visualize getting a promo-

> *So be mindful what you dream, as well has how you pursue your dream.*

tion? Do you need to imagine your future house? The more detail, the better.

Use self-talk and visualization together to program your unconscious mind. Get your unconscious to work on these problems for you. The unconscious mind is always at work. If your subconscious CLEARLY knows what you want, it will continually work hard to find a way for you to achieve your goals. You may even wake up with answers because your mind has worked on the problem while you were asleep! Countless people have reported waking up with their best ideas. Your subconscious mind already works day and night. We are just encouraging you to help direct that natural process. Make it work more effectively for you.

So, like self-talk, visualization is something you already do, but can probably do better. It has been said that "Your mind thinks much better in pictures than in words." Picture achieving your goals and dreams in your mind's eye. This technique is used by essentially all highly successful people. People don't become lawyers, doctors, public speakers, and successful business people without first imagining themselves doing it. The trick is to enhance and gain more control on your visualizations.

Imagine every detail that you can about your specific dream(s). What would owning your own business feel like? What would you produce or what services would you provide. Where would it be located? What would your office look like? Have you gone into a furniture store and imaged which office furniture you will buy? How many staff would you want to employ and how would you want them to think about you? Would you have a cherry desk? What would your chair look like? Would it be leather? What would you do with all the money you will make? How will your wife or husband feel about your success? How will you celebrate with them? Get to the level of detail that truly excites and motives you. Make your dream one that you enjoy thinking and dreaming about.

If your dream is to be a doctor, firefighter, teacher, lawyer, athlete, coach, or business person, then go talk to them. Be around them. Former Mayor Bill Campbell of Atlanta, before he was mayor, often had his picture taken with the honorable Maynard Jackson and Andrew Young. Both of these men had been mayors. Guess what? Campbell became the mayor of Atlanta and served two terms. Volunteer to help people you admire or who do jobs that you would like to do. Not only will being in their environment help clarify your visualization of success, but it may bring you connections to help achieve that success! What better place to get recommendations than from people at the place you want to work or from people who are already recognized in the field. For example, Dr. Hubbard has known many pre-med college students who volunteered to do research or clinical work at medical schools. In many cases the experience and connections helped them get into medical school. In some cases you may discover that your dream was not all that it was cracked up to be. That is okay. Now you can re-evaluate the direction you want to go. You can develop a new and better dream. But whatever your dream(s) may be, find inspiration and develop a clearer picture of success by being around it.

To achieve your dreams you will need to achieve many short-term goals. Picture yourself accomplishing your smaller goals, too. Some of these goals may include completing a difficult college course, eliminating your debt, or developing new skills and connections. See yourself doing it. Achieving these smaller goals can be half the fun. Sometimes a dream takes many years, if not a lifetime, to achieve. So enjoy your smaller successes along the way as well! Take a few minutes and reflect by writing out some of the small successes you have already achieved. Then write out some goals you want to achieve. If you take time to do this, you are working this book of Pearls. Completing short-term goals will bring you confidence and inch you steadily forward toward fulfilling your dream(s).

The goals you select should be part of your larger plan. If they are not, you may waste years going in a direction that takes you nowhere. This often happens when people get caught up in other people's goals and dreams that are not their own. So get your self-talk, visualization, and planning (an upcoming Pearl) all working in the same direction. Try not to just visualize who you have been, envision who you CAN BE! Life is too short to put off moving towards your dreams.

Tim McCormick, a former NBA player, tells high school students in the All American Basketball Players Clinic (of the National Basketball Player's Association summer camp) to hold on to their dreams. He asks, "How many times have you had a wonderful dream and suddenly you woke up and couldn't get back to the same dream?" Many hands go up. That is what happens to many people who start out with a wonderful dream, get sidetracked or allow others to sidetrack them. So he reminds them to watch out for the "sidetrackers in your life."

Finally, help your children develop their dreams. Cherish your children by teaching them how to set goals. Several years ago Earl Suttle attended a seminar on goal setting. The seminar leader instructed those in attendance to go back to their homes and ask their children to do a goal setting follow-up assignment. Earl agreed to follow the suggestion and went back to speak to his younger daughter Zani. At the time, she was eleven years old. About a year earlier his wife, Felicia, who is South African, had been asked by Nelson Mandela to return home to South Africa to help in the rebuilding of South Africa (because of their recent independence). This left Earl alone in the U.S. with his daughters Lindi and Zani. His daughter Zani seemed very eager to do this assignment of goal setting. She said, "Daddy what are goals?" He told her goals are nothing more than those things you desire to accomplish (in her case) in school and tennis. At the time, his daughter had just started playing in a lot of tennis tournaments and he felt it was a good time to help her think about what she wanted to accomplish in that sport. So, she decided to go in her room and write out what she considered to be her dreams. She came back about twenty minutes later and had a list of things she wanted to accomplish. Below is the list she came up with:

FAMILY GOALS:

To try and get this family back together.

To hope that Mommy's two jobs are good.

To get Daddy a real job that he would like.

To visit the Bahamas, Hong Kong, Japan, Canada, and Nigeria.

SCHOOL GOALS:

To get all A's in every subject this quarter.

To help get Lindi to go to college.

TENNIS GOALS:

To be #1 in the state of Georgia in the 12-and-under age group.

To be #1 in the South.

To help get Lindi a tennis scholarship.

To be a pro.

OTHER GOALS:

To have a birthday party when Mommy is here.

To make my birthday party be the best birthday ever.

To hope Mommy has a safe flight in Atlanta and back to South Africa.

To get heat in Lindi's car.

To hope that Mommy will be safe in South Africa
  at all times.

To write a letter to Mommy at least 3 times a month.

OTHER:

TO BE A MILLIONAIRE!

* * * *

Earl was astonished by the list she put together. She even added some family goals which they had never discussed previously. At first it ticked Earl off a little when he read that she wanted him to get a "real job." At the time he had quit his full-time job as director of an outpatient substance abuse program and decided to start his own business as a consultant. She never thought that being a consultant was a real job. Earl reviewed the list with her. That night, when he went to her room to kiss her goodnight, he noticed she had drawn on her wall "A and number 1." Earl said, "Zani, why did you do that?" She replied, "Daddy, when I go to sleep I want to dream about getting these, and when I wake up I want to see these before I go to school each day." Earl thought to himself, "Kids will do incredibly creative things if you give them the opportunity and create an atmosphere for it to happen." Later that month in the first marking period, Zani had all A's except for one B. Earl remembers her saying, "Daddy, I almost did it!" The second marking period she had all A's. Wow! That summer she was competing in the state Junior Tennis Tournament for girls 12 and under in Macon, Georgia. Usually the player who wins that important tournament will be recognized as the number one player in the state that year. In that tournament, Zani didn't finish number one, nor did she finish number two. But she finished third, which is pretty good for first-time goal setting!

Earl learned, for probably the first time, the true power of goal setting. His daughter also learned how important it was to write down her dreams. Since then, not only Zani, but also Earl's entire family set goals where they write out their dreams for the year. Earl says his wife Felicia has become the family's best goal setter. She has learned to carry the dreams that she has written down with her in her purse and frequently refers to them. She also publicly shares them with her audiences when she delivers her motivational speeches on attitude and shares with them readers of her recent book *Dare to Dream*. Goal setting can change lives.

You might say, I don't have time to do goal setting. That is a cop-out. Steve Chandler in his book *"100 Ways to Motivate Yourself"* has a short term method for goal setting. He says you can successfully set goals in just four minutes. He says all you do is make four large circles on a sheet of paper. Write over each circle the words "I want." Over the first circle write, "I want today." Over the second circle write, "I want for the month". Over the third circle write, "I want for the year." Over the last circle write, "I want in a lifetime." Just quickly put in each circle what you want to accomplish. Do this exercise now as you read this Pearl and see what happens. Remarkable results suddenly will begin to occur in your life.

* * * *

TRY THESE IDEAS:

1. Clearly visualize the 1, 2, or 3 biggest dreams in your life.

2. Write down three goals that you want to accomplish this year. Make them in different parts of your life.

3. Write down three goals or dreams you want to accomplish in the next three years, in the next five years, and in the next ten years. Re-read these regularly. Visualize your success.

* * * *

Suggested Affirmation: Say out loud 10 times, "My mind thinks more in pictures than words, so I am visualizing my dreams every day."

* * * *

Write down the most important thing(s) to remember from this Pearl:

_____

_____

_____

_____

PEARL #7

&

Plan, Plan, Plan

*"One important key to success is self-confidence.
An important key to self-confidence is preparation."*
—Arthur Ashe

*"Give a man health and a course to steer,
and he'll never stop to trouble about
whether he's happy or not."*
—George Bernard Shaw

*"A wise man will make more opportunities
than he finds."*
—Francis Bacon

* * * *

KAWANISH ROSS, a master junior tennis coach in Atlanta, was talking to a young tennis player about preparing to hit the ball. The student had difficulty understanding Coach Ross' point. Coach Ross then gave the puzzled student two examples of preparation. He said, "Before you go to school what do you have to do?"

The student said, "Well, eat breakfast, put on some clothes, get my books, and have my assignments together in my backpack."

The coach then asked him, "If you have a test, what do you have to do before the test?"

The student replied, "Well, I have to study first." The student looked at the tennis teacher and said, "Oh, I got it!" You should have seen how this kid got more prepared to hit the tennis ball in that lesson.

As stated so well by Benjamin Franklin, "By failing to prepare you are preparing to fail." To be successful you have to develop a PLAN. After all, your goals and dreams are too important to be left to chance, blind luck, or to other people. *Being without a plan is like being in a boat without a rudder and letting the current take you wherever it chooses.* You don't want your life to just drift along or find yourself going over a waterfall. You need a plan for success. Many people are just drifting along without a plan for their life. Being without a plan may add many extra years to achieving your dreams. Or worse, you may never achieve them at all. So make a road map to follow. Making plans helps you take control of your life and refuels the energy within you.

> *Being without a plan is like being in a boat without a rudder and letting the current take you wherever it chooses.*

So where do you begin? Start with the dreams and goals that you developed in the previous Pearl. Stay focused on those dreams and goals so that they become a part of you. Review them often. Discuss your dreams, goals, and plans with your spouse and children. Get everyone excited and on the same page. Develop a step-wise plan so that you can cut through obstacles (and there are always many) like a laser beam. Have comprehensive plans to improve many important areas of your life, including your family, health, wealth, and spiritual direction. In a John Maxwell workshop on leadership, he asked the audience, "Do you have a personal growth plan?" Very few people raised their hand. At the time, Earl was one of those people who didn't raise his hand because he had not written a personal growth plan anywhere. Earl left that workshop determined to put his plan together. Below is Earl's everyday plan that he adopted from Maxwell's workshop. Earl shares it with you in this book to help you get started if you don't already have a plan.

EARL'S PERSONAL GROWTH PLAN

1. Everyday I listen to audiotapes on motivation, leadership, communication, finance, or relationships (at least one hour). I listen while driving in my car.

2. Every morning I read something inspirational and motivational (i.e., the Bible, Iyanla Vanzant's *Acts of Faith*, or a daily meditation book).

3. Every morning I take a brisk walk to start my day off with a victory! Yes, I take an audiotape player with me each time and listen while I walk. This is called "blending" (combining exercise and learning). By doing this, I complete two of my objectives as once.

4. I attend at least one workshop or seminar per month. If I can't get to a workshop, I go to a bookstore and purchase a book (that's my workshop for the month).

5. Each week I speak to a motivated person.

6. I file something important in my diary each day.

7. Each month I buy a book and give it away to somebody I think will benefit from reading it. Because I have pro-

duced motivational tapes over the years, I usually give away motivational tapes of my seminars.

* * * *

How is your *health*? Where do you need to improve most? What plan do you need to improve your health? Do you need to stop smoking, reduce that beer belly or tone your legs? Visualize the health and body shape you want. Use positive self-talk to reprogram your self image to the new you. Develop a plan to slowly but steadily move in that direction. Put your plan into action and develop health promoting habits. Find a way to stop smoking. Cigarettes can drastically harm your health even if they don't kill you. You may not get lung cancer, but having to stop to catch your breath after walking a flight of stairs is no fun. Consider reducing your alcohol intake if you drink more than one or two drinks a day. In excess, alcohol can be toxic to just about every part of your body. Dr. Hubbard is a physician and addiction specialist who has written about the many ways alcohol (and other drugs) harm the mind and body (see *Primary Care Medicine For Specialists and Non-Specialists* and *Substance Abuse in the Mentally and Physically Disabled* in the bibliography).

Everyone needs exercise, especially aerobic exercise (such as brisk walking, cycling, tennis, jogging, or stairmaster-like machines). Try to work out at least 30 minutes three to six days a week. You'll feel great. We suggest brisk walking first. Weightlifting of some sort is best for shaping muscles and some form of walking, running, or swimming adds more to your general health. Exercise is good clean fun that will help your body, mind, and self-image more than you can image. It also becomes a great way to pamper yourself. Dr. Hubbard and his wife Suzanne use exercise (about 4 to 6 times a week) not only to stay fit, but also as a major way to relax. Most people don't pamper themselves enough. Pamper yourself with regular exercise. You will not regret it.

Do you have a plan for *financial success*? Being rich does not make you a better person or a worse one. Having money does, however, reduce many of the stresses in people's lives and can empower you to help others in new ways. Countless marriages struggle or even break up each year largely because of financial stress. Again, develop a plan to ease this burden by earning more money and cutting back where you can. Plan a way out of debt (if you need to) and into solid savings. Try to develop a safety net for when you are ill or if you lose your job. Many people advise having a savings account to cover at least three months salary. This gives you time to find a new job if you lose your current one unexpectedly.

Write down your plan for financial success. Money won't come to you without planning and effort. Develop plans to have multiple sources of income. Put your money to work through sound investments. Try to develop an income that keeps coming to you after most of the work has been done. This could entail owning your own business or perhaps being successful in the stock market. You will find out that it is mostly YOU holding you back from achieving financial dreams. The Bible warns of the dangers of the *love* of money (not money itself), so be careful. Money should not rule over you, but you should rule over your money. Like any powerful force, money can be used for good or bad purposes. Use your wealth for good purposes and obtain it by honest means. There is no true happiness with it otherwise.

If you are *married* or have a steady relationship, think about ways to have the best marriage (or relationship) you can. Imagine ways to make your spouse thankful that he or she married you. Clarify to one another your expectations of marriage. Marriage is both social and spiritual by nature. Try reading the Bible and discuss it together in order to clarify God's meaning and plan for marriage. Marriage based on biblical principles is vital for getting through hard times. Having a solid marriage is a great blessing, and having a struggling one can bring people to despair. Try not to judge your spouse harshly; instead, work more on what YOU can do to vitalize or revitalize your marriage. What a joy it is to have a fulfilling marriage and what happiness it is to know you are being a great husband or wife to your spouse.

Remember, marriage is not easy. But the more you put into it, the more value it is to you. God does not create your problems, but some difficulties present the opportunity for spiritual development and a closer relationship with God. What you get from a relationship is mostly what you give. You can only control what *you* think and do. Are you giving enough in your marriage? Do you show your spouse how thankful you are to be married to her or him? Plan a way to improve your marriage (or close relationships). Take time to make each other feel appreciated. Give each other small gifts and plan time alone together. Be sure your marriage has a strong spiritual foundation because the world will surely throw many obstacles at the two of you.

Make plans to improve your *spiritual life*. You are more than mere flesh and bone. You have a spirit that needs nurturing too. Your body will not last forever, but your spirit can. When times are really hard the need for spiritual faith becomes all too evident. Plan ways to grow spiritually so that you won't look back on your life with regret. Read the Bible and whatever other books inspire your spiritual growth. Pray often. Trust that God loves you and has provided ways for you to get through any difficulty. Plan to be around spiritual people who care about you. Those with strong faith are those most resilient to the turmoil of the world. It all works together: body, mind and spirit.

We can learn a lot from ants. Ants always think about winter during the summer. Have you ever heard of "Earlsop's Fable" about the ant and grasshopper? (It's modern-day version of Aesop's classic fable.) One day an ant was planning for the winter and a grasshopper was sitting on the side of the road laughing at the ant. The grasshopper tried to make the ant feel bad, but the ant didn't go for it. When the winter came, guess what happened? Yes, the grasshopper died because he did not prepare for winter. *Then the ant ate him*! Try not to be like the grasshopper. Be like the ant. Ants are always planning and working hard. As the old saying goes, if you are not planning, you are planning to fail. If you are not a planner, you will be fit into someone else's plans. And guess what somebody else has planned for you? Something for them! So be a planner. Think things through and be sure that the plans you develop are consistent with plans God has for you.

In their audiotape series for The People's Network (TPN), well-known parenting specialists and experts in life balance Richard and Linda Eyre recommend that each month both husband and wife should have a couple's meeting away from their children and write out on a sheet of paper the following words:

Physically

Mentally

Socially

Emotionally

Spiritually

Both parents then discuss and assess how each of the children are doing in each of these areas. As they go down the list, they ask each other, "How is our son or daughter doing physically, mentally, socially, emotionally, and spiritually?" They quickly assess each area and if they have a concern with one area, that becomes the area of focus for the parents that month. If you are a single parent, you may have to do this exercise alone or with a friend who knows your children well.

* * * *

TRY THESE IDEAS:

1. Develop a plan to improve your health. Walk, jog, play tennis, or basketball. Work on your health at least 30 minutes three to five days a week. Who will benefit? You will and you'll love it.

2. Develop a plan to improve your love relationships. How can you better let your wife, husband, or other loved one know how much you love and care about them? Don't let old baggage get in the way. Your husband or wife is far too important for that (and so are you).

3. Do you need more money? Develop one, three, five, and ten year plans to fulfill your financial goals. Money isn't everything, but if you don't have to worry so much about money it sure is easier to focus on other aspects of your life.

4. Develop a plan to grow spiritually. Set aside time to read the Bible each day. Be sure to pray and stay in harmony with God's plans for you.

* * * *

Suggested Affirmation: Say out loud 10 times, "I am writing out my personal growth plan, customized for me alone, and I am following it everyday."

* * * *

Write down the most important thing(s) to remember from this Pearl:

_____

_____

_____

PEARL # 8

Learn to Laugh (Especially at Yourself)

"Laughter is the best medicine."
—Proverb

"I love myself when I'm laughing."
—Zora Neale Hurston

"Seven days without laughter makes one weak."
—Anonymous

* * * *

AT A LEADERSHIP SEMINAR Earl attended, he heard about a way to describe different kinds of people. It went something like this. Pick the symbol that best represents you: a triangle, square, or circle. Think for a moment now, and decide on a symbol for you. Have you picked one? If you picked a triangle you are highly intelligent. If you chose a square, you are highly creative. Finally, if you picked the circle you are a very sexy person. Now our question to you is: How badly would you like to change your answer to the circle?

What can laughter do for you? What is the connection between laughter and your success? First of all, laughter can help change your perception on things. Laughter helps take the edge off of your problems and can enhance the learning process. It helps you bond with the people that laugh with you. People like to be around people who have a good sense of humor and can make others laugh. It is a connecting point with people and helps relationships. Some scientists say laughter puts more oxygen in the brain. It calms your body. It helps reduce your stress.

Life is full of stress. Sometimes stress can make you feel overwhelmed. As described in Dr. Hubbard's book *Stress Medicine: an Organ System Approach*, a considerable amount of scientific and clinical data already exists showing that severe stress can damage many, if not all, parts of your body. High stress (more appropriately called "distress") increases the risk and severity of headaches, chest pain (angina), upper respiratory infections, neck pain, skin problems, back pain, diarrhea, and many other physical illnesses. High stress can also affect your emotional state leading to (or worsening) anxiety, panic attacks, depression, substance abuse, and/or relationship problems. Stress appears to attack people at their individual weak point(s). Because everyone is different, stress manifests itself in different ways. For that reason, high stress may cause one person to have headaches, another to have diarrhea, and a third person angina.

So what can you do about your stress? Actually, there are many ways to reduce stress, such as exercise, increasing relaxation time, taking an overdue vacation with your spouse, reflecting more, and remembering to laugh often. Perhaps the most natural, and simplest, place to start is laughter. As author Barbara Johnson has said, "Love makes the world go 'round , but laughter keeps you from getting dizzy." Countless people have become overburdened with money problems, work stress, raising children, caring for an elderly parent, and a thousand other things. In short, many people are too busy to laugh. It is very important that you learn to laugh more even if times are tough. Be confident that you can handle life's problems and try to laugh whenever you can. As Mother Teresa said, "I know God won't give me more than I can handle. I just wish he didn't trust me so much." Do you feel that way sometimes?

You may be thinking that you have nothing to laugh about. Everybody's circumstances are different and we have no desire to minimize your problems. However, there may be more to laugh about than you realize. Let's get creative for a moment. For example, watch how adults interact differently with children. In fact, it has been said that children laugh on average about ten times more a day than adults. One parent or teacher may go nuts and pull out their hair because of the wild behavior of a small child. Yet another teacher or parent may laugh themselves silly at the special nature of this same child. Dr. Hubbard's daughter, Tara Reid, recently shared with him the thoughts of some of her elementary school students. With her permission we will share them with you. (Thanks, Tara!) See if you don't agree that children can be hysterical:

> **On the birth of his sister:** "She was covered with jelly and butter. And thank goodness I'm not a girl. They have a garden hose coming out of their bellies."

> **On relationships:** "I have two boyfriends, but one doesn't know it yet."

> **When asked to get some tissue for his nose:** "Oh, its just snot. I'll get it with my fingernail later on."

> **When told how smart he is:** "Trust me, I know!"

In a letter to Tara's fiancé (Lt. Aaron Reid): "I hope you enjoy Ms. Hubbard."

* * * *

So laughter is less about what is going on around you than how you chose to react to it. Choose to smile and laugh more often. Try to see the humor in your weaknesses, mistakes, and other aspects of your life. Take the time to laugh at the adventures of children and the funny behaviors of pets. A dog or a cat can bring a lot of laughter to a home.

Did you know that the brain is unable to sustain two opposite emotions at the same time? Why is that important to remember? Because it is therefore nearly impossible to laugh and feel anxious or depressed at the same time! Try feeling depressed while you are laughing. You can't. Perhaps this is why athletes and other high intensity performers often make jokes just before a big game. Laughter relieves stress, and stress reduction helps you relax and perform at your best.

> *So laughter is less about what is going on around you than how you chose to react to it.*

Use humor not only to relieve your stress, but also to reduce stress in people around you. Your family and coworkers (or employees) probably need a little stress reduction, too. Here is one important **WARNING:** The humor and laughter we are discussing is that which enhances joy for yourself and other people. It does not include critical personal sarcasm and other forms of degrading humor that deliberately hurts other people. You know the difference. Can you remember being the brunt of rude jokes because of your weight, nose, hair, body shape, or perhaps the color of your skin? We have all been hurt at some time by these so-called jokes. This type of humor may seem harmless enough, but it can be very destructive. Remember, differently cultured groups have different sensitivities. People can recall the hurt and embarrassment they experienced as the object of someone's joke—even 20 or 30 years after the joke is made. Delivering harsh sarcasm is a form of one-upsmanship that, no matter how benign it may try to appear, is actually a poorly disguised cruel act. In fact, the Bible has many strict warnings about the evils of the tongue. On the other hand, good-hearted laughter is fun, healthy, and can add years to your life. Laughter will enhance your health, emotions, spirit, and relationships. Interestingly, it is not unusual for overly stressed or depressed people to say, "I just want to be able to laugh again."

So how do you learn to laugh more? Let's continue with some more creative thinking. Perhaps you need to reflect back on what things make you laugh. What sort of things did you find funny? Do you need to be around small children to laugh more? Grandchildren, nieces and nephews can be a delight. Maybe you need to visit them. Do you like slapstick humor in movies? Have you rented a comedy lately? Learning to laugh again may mean LETTING GO of old regrets and bitterness. Resentments hold you back and hold your laughter back. A good thing to laugh at is yourself! People are pretty funny. People get upset over little things and neglect the important stuff. Learn to laugh at yourself, and others won't laugh at you.

Laughter often comes from being around other people who laugh a lot. Listen to morning talk radio and you will find that some people are actually paid to laugh. A funny talk show host is made much more funny by having a person (or people) in the studio who readily laugh at everything he says. Television shows put in laughter sound tracks to help make you laugh. Have you ever been in a room when someone started laughing hysterically and found that soon the whole room was laughing too?

So find people who laugh easily and be around them. Often these are people who have common interests or shared experiences such as children, school, or sports. Start telling stories about growing up with people who grew up under similar circumstances and watch how quickly all of you begin laughing. Let two grown men or women get together who haven't seen each other for many years and soon you'll have two boys or girls laughing and playing. Let a group of tired and overburdened young mothers get together and soon you'll see them laughing at things that would have made them cry just a few moments before. It is important to be around nice people that laugh with you, not at you. Laugh with your children and with your husband or wife. If you don't laugh enough with your spouse, perhaps the two of you need to get away from all of life's tensions and relax a little. Raising a family can be hard work. But be careful not to make it all work. You will soon be laughing together again once you take time to have some fun and relaxation together.

Laughter and good humor are amazingly powerful tools that reduce your tension and the tension of people around you.

Sometimes laughter comes from doing goofy things or something very different from your usual day. For some people this may mean going dancing again. Others have a grand time at comedy clubs, water parks, sports events, whitewater rafting, hiking, cycling, or going to an amusement park. Be creative. It has been said that "Angels fly because they take themselves lightly." Make opportunities to laugh and use laughter and humor to enhance your life. *Laughter and good humor are amazingly powerful tools that reduce your tension and the tension of people around you.* Laughter heals, reduces anger, and refreshes. It will add to your life. In this way excellence is easier to achieve, and you will have more fun achieving it. We will leave you with this old saying, "If you can learn to laugh at your problems, you will never stop laughing."

* * * *

TRY THESE IDEAS:

1. Surprise your wife or husband with a special smile today. Smile as often as you can. It is a step close to laughter.

2. Share a funny story or a good joke with a friend, your child, or with your husband or wife.

3. Watch a funny movie tonight and attend a comic relief show in your community. Find one that makes you laugh out loud.

4. Try to see the humor in things. Children's behaviors can be a terrible headache if you expect them to act like adults, or they can be really funny as you watch them grow and learn.

* * * *

Suggested Affirmation: Say out loud 10 times, "I am laughing more and allowing the child to come out of me more often."

* * * *

Write down the most important thing(s) to remember from this Pearl:

_____

_____

_____

PEARL # 9

Avoid the "I'll Be Happy When" Syndrome

"Be ready when opportunity comes…Luck is the time when preparation and opportunity meet."
—Roy D. Chaplin, Jr.

"Growl all day and you'll feel dog tired at night."
—Anonymous

"It's not so much the decision you make, but what you make of your decision."
—Dr. John Hubbard

* * * *

HAVE YOU HEARD OF THE OLD "I'll Be Happy When" syndrome? It is an illness that can destroy relationships, disrupt families, hinder success at work, and cause people to miss out on a lot of happiness. You know how this one goes. "I'll be happy when I graduate from school." You graduate from school and then what do you say? "I'll be happy when I land a good job." After you get the good job what do you say? "I'll be happy when I have a better job." You land a better job and what do you say? "I'll be happy when I retire!" What is wrong with this picture? What is wrong is that too many people keep waiting to be content and happy. They need to allow themselves to be happy *now*. As legendary UCLA basketball coach John Wooden said, "Make each day your masterpiece." *You must **decide** to be happy **now**, even if times are tough. People should not wait for the time when all their stresses have disappeared, because that will never happen! Life always has stresses whether you are old or young, rich or poor.* Happiness is an *attitude*, not a state of circumstances. Sure, there may be easier times down the road, but try to find some internal peace, thankfulness, and joy now, as well.

> *You must **decide** to be happy **now**, even if times are tough. People should not wait for the time when all their stresses have disappeared, because that will never happen! Life always has stresses whether you are old or young, rich or poor.*

There are a million examples of the "I'll Be Happy When" syndrome. What is yours? Is it "I'll be happy when I get *more* money"? Then after you get more money, you need more money. Perhaps it is the search for the perfect man or woman. "I'll be happy when a great man (or woman) comes along." Perhaps it is obtaining the perfect figure. "I'll be happy when I fit into a size 5, 8, or 10 again." Have you found yourself in any of these examples yet? Can you envision how your trap will play out? Here are just a few other common examples that you may identify with. "I'll be happy when I get married." After you get married, what do you say? "I'll be happy when I have children." What happens next? "Boy, I'll be happy when the children are grown." And finally, far too many people these days think, "I'll be happy when I'm single again!" People get on these roads to misery without even noticing what has happened to them or why. But be sure, the "I'll Be Happy When" syndrome does lead to misery.

Roger Mellot, in his audiotape series "Stress Management for Professionals" describes a toothpaste commercial: a woman confides to her friend, "Honey, I can't find a man." The other woman replies, "Well, honey, why don't you brush your teeth with [name brand] toothpaste?" And guess what? She brushes her teeth with that particular toothpaste and finds the perfect man! Wouldn't it be nice to just brush your teeth and get what you want in life? Many people have become addicted to this simplistic mentality. They think life should be easy, simple and always happy. But in truth, life is often stressed. That does not mean that you cannot be happy. It just means that you must find a great attitude and happiness now. We are not talking about quick fix forms of happiness that may eventually lead to hurt. Some quick fixes lead to such dangers as spending sprees you can't afford, fast and reckless driving, extramarital affairs, and drug abuse. Many other behaviors lead to similar destruction. Instead, find happiness—and true joy—by doing what is right and deciding not to dwell on what makes you feel anxious, angry, or sad.

Think back for a moment. Each time when you got something you wanted you were happy for a short time, but soon you found a new set of problems or desires, didn't you? This seems to be a part of human nature. However, with effort, this can be minimized by reminding yourself that happiness is primarily an ATTITUDE, not a possession. Because it is an attitude, it can be maintained more easily than by finding new toys or other pleasures. Rich people can be terribly sad, and poor folks can be very happy. Money helps bring security and freedom to enjoy certain things, but only a good attitude brings contentment and true happiness. Happiness can be a walk in the park or a good book. The attitude of "I'll be happy when" can turn into "poor me...poor me... poor me." And by the time some people get to the ninth "poor me," they say "pour me a drink." That is how some people start drinking heavily, isn't it? Too many people are alcoholics in part as a result of feeling sorry for themselves and viewing themselves as victims in life.

Don't be too discouraged if you suffer from the "I'll Be Happy When Syndrome" because you have a lot of company. Everyone catches the "I'll Be Happy When" virus now and then. But make it a short-lived infection and try not to let it become a chronic illness. The cure to this illness is to *decide* you will be content and happy *now*. The Bible emphasizes to have faith and to be content with your blessings. Perhaps you may need to take a time-out and truly count your blessings. Do it right now. Write them down. Isn't it a shame to wait for happiness? Joy is an attitude that you can have right now. Don't make it into a carrot hanging out on a stick in front of you that you can never reach. Be ready and willing to embrace happiness today. Society promotes discontent because it is by discontent that people can sell you something. If people were content they wouldn't need a new car, a bigger TV, or a thousand other things.

Do you know why TODAY is the best day of your life? It is the best day because it is the only day you have! Yesterday is gone and who really knows what tomorrow will bring. As the saying goes, "Yesterday is history, tomorrow is a mystery, but today is a gift. That's why they call today the present." This book is about finding ways to improve your life, but also how to be content along the journey. Try not wait for happiness to come to you. As we said in Pearl #1, you take responsibility for your happiness. Take responsibility for a happy attitude.

The movie "Groundhog Day" is a wonderful illustration of how any day can be the worst day of your life or your best day, depending on what you do with it. In the film a man mystically gets stuck living the same day (Groundhog Day) over and over again. Depending on his attitude and his behaviors, the same day (initially identical in all other ways) could be so bad that he was suicidal, or so wonderful that he found the love of his life and was adored by an entire town. Try not to let the day control you. You can control each day. Decide to be thankful, giving, and happy NOW.

* * * *

TRY THESE IDEAS:

1. Reflect on your "I'll be happy when" habits. Write them down, tear up the paper and decide that it will not become a habit or chronic illness.

2. Try deciding that you will have a good time the next time you go out, rather than waiting to see if you have a good time.

3. Tell someone today how happy you are. You may shock them. If you are married, tell your husband or wife that they make you happy. Try not to wait until everything is perfect. They will appreciate it more than you could imagine!

* * * *

Suggested Affirmation: Say out loud 10 times, "This moment feels good because I am finding more ways to look at life differently."

* * * *

Write down the most important thing(s) to remember from this Pearl:

_____

_____

_____

_____

PEARL #10

Bounce Back From Your Failures

"Be like a tennis ball; learn to bounce back."
—Felicia Suttle

"I am not discouraged, because every wrong attempt discarded is another step forward."
—Thomas Edison

"Failure isn't so bad if it doesn't attack the heart. Success is all right if it doesn't attack the heart."
—Grantland Rice

* * * *

NO ONE WANTS TO FAIL, but we all do. When Earl conducts seminars all over the USA he takes a lot of tennis balls in a large bag to throw out to the participants, reminding them that they have to learn to bounce back from bad things that happen to them. People put out their hands, wanting to catch a ball, and have a great feeling of excitement when they do. Many will drop the ball and pick it up

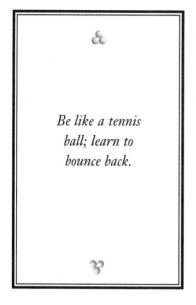

Be like a tennis ball; learn to bounce back.

again. Then all of a sudden, Earl takes out of his bag two very large, oversized tennis balls and the participants go wild, clamoring for the gigantic tennis balls. Many people will get out of their seat and run up to get a larger ball. He reminds them that this is the enthusiasm they will need to have about life, and the enthusiasm that will attract others to them. That sort of enthusiasm will help them to bounce back faster from their mishaps. Earl tells them that most problems in life are not setbacks, but are mishaps that they can recover from. One woman attending a seminar who caught one of the tennis balls called Earl back later. She said each time she had a difficult day at work she would go into her office, close the door, get out her tennis ball, and bounce it several times, reminding herself that she needs to bounce back and regroup. Earl further recalls after another seminar, a woman came up to him and quietly asked him, "Can I please have a tennis ball? I have a friend who is dying of cancer and I want to take it to her. I hope giving her this ball will cheer her up and give her more hope and encouragement to keep fighting for her life." She went away holding onto the ball tightly with a smile on her face. Earl recalls another touching situation at the close of one of his seminars where a teenager approached him and said, "Can I have a tennis ball? I love your exercise about the tennis balls. My father just lost his job, and we are in a bad way right now. I want to give it to him and encourage him to bounce back." She looked very sad and had tears in her eyes as she asked Earl. He gave her two tennis balls instead of one and autographed them with the inscription, "Never give up." Earl now brings loads of tennis balls in a large NBA bag to all of his seminars. It becomes one of the most inspirational parts of his seminars, teaching his audiences the need to bounce back and keep their enthusiasm in life. (Thanks, Felicia for the tennis ball idea.) The only way you can't make mistakes is not to try. As the U.S. diplomat Edward John Phelps said, "The man who makes no mistakes does not usually make anything." So if you try, sometimes you will make mistakes. And if you make mistakes you must bounce back from them.

Do you realize that your failures can be your friends? Failures do not have to lead to your demise. Although it is easier said than done, it is true that successful people know how to make the most of their failures. Failure is just one step closer to success. Basketball great Michael Jordan has said, "I have failed over and over again, that's why I succeed." In fact, failure probably means you were bold enough to take a risk or two. How many times does a baby fall before he or she can walk? If parents didn't let them fall they would never learn how to walk. Failure means that you have learned something or should have learned something. Watch great quarterbacks like Brett Favre, Donovan McNabb, and Peyton Manning. They take chances and make mistakes. But their boldness has also led them to become outstanding NFL quarterbacks who are rich, famous, and respected. They get intercepted a lot, but they don't let their interceptions stop them from throwing the next pass or the next touchdown. At halftime, football teams evaluate their mistakes. Those teams that learn from their first half mistakes make adjustments and play better in the second half. Unfortunately, what happens to some people when they fail is that they become depressed. Do you fade away after failure, or do

Courage to face possible failure again is what allows people to succeed.

you throw the next pass? You must work on getting out of your box after a mistake if you want to be successful. Courage to face possible failure again is what allows people to succeed.

Failures and mistakes happen in all areas of life. In fact, Marianne Williamson (a renowned motivational speaker and minister) said people shouldn't call them "failures." Rather, they are only brief learning experiences that help you grow. Sometimes it is the mistakes at home that hurt us the most. All marriages have their share of poor communication, mistakes, and setbacks. As such, marriage provides us with constant learning opportunities. That may be one reason God made the genders different—to learn (and need) one another. Those of you who have been married for many years can easily think back on all that you have learned over the years. Although you cannot turn back the clock, this experience should be used to prevent future problems and to teach or set an example for younger couples (such as your children) who are still learning. Once again, as in Pearl #1, take responsibility for your failure, learn from your mistakes, and be resolved to do better in the future.

There are many examples of successful people who knew the value of learning from their mistakes. One of the best examples was the great American inventor, Thomas Edison. It is said that he had about 10,000 failures before he finally invented the light bulb! And that was the number of failures he endured for only *one* of his inventions! He had many other inventions and failures. Who else would have kept going after 10, 100, 1,000 or 2,000 failures? How did he do it? He had a dream, visualized that dream, and had the right attitude towards failure. Edison said that each failure taught him something. After 10,000 failures on the light bulb he became the wisest man in the world on the subject! His determination and willingness to learn from his mistakes were rewarded with great financial success for himself and better and safer lighting for the rest of the world. As a nation, the U.S. learned a lot from our failures in Vietnam. Our country learned the importance of national consent when going to war, the importance of victory when we do, and many ideas about waging that sort of battle. The lessons the U.S. learned in Vietnam clearly helped in the Persian Gulf War victory and more recently in Afghanistan.

Viewing failure as a learning process also helps you keep a positive attitude in hard times. You must DECIDE if failure is going to make you depressed or if it is going to be your teacher. If you become depressed, withdrawn, or develop low self-confidence after a failure the road back to success will be much more difficult. There is nothing wrong with a short period of disappointment after failure. That is normal. But consider failure as part of your education. It can enhance your energy, rather than drain you of it.

What failures have you had recently? What failures are acting as your teacher today? Did you lose confidence at work when something didn't go the way you wanted it to? Have you been too harsh with your children or spouse and felt bad about it later? Take a moment and think about what you learned from your failures. Say no to being a cynic. Some people may say, "I learned that I am an idiot," or "I learned that I'm a jerk," or "I learned that I am a failure." Is that how you want to program your mind? Is that how you want to see yourself in your mind's eye? You can't afford to beat yourself up like that. Reflect on your mistakes. Forgive yourself, learn, and make adjustments from what you've learned.

Failing is not being a failure. Was Thomas Edison a failure? Excellence does not mean being "perfect." Learn from your mis-

Failing is not being a failure.

takes. The more you can do this the faster you will accomplish your dreams and the more you will enjoy your life.

* * * *

TRY THESE IDEAS:

1. Reflect on how you handled your last failure. How could you have reacted better? What did you learn from the problem? What could you do differently next time?

2. Be determined not to let your failures beat you. Decide that you will learn from them to keep moving forward.

3. Remind yourself that failing is not being a failure.

* * * *

Suggested Affirmation: Say out loud 10 times, "I am bouncing back from my failures like a tennis ball. My failures are my teachers."

* * * *

Write down the most important thing(s) to remember from this Pearl:

_____

_____

_____

_____

PEARL #11

Have Faith

*"Believe you are defeated, believe it long enough
and it is likely to become a fact."*
—Norman Vincent Peale

*"Your beliefs are your reality. If you don't like
the reality you see, change your beliefs."*
—Stephen C. Paul

*"I tell you the truth, if you have faith as small
as a mustard seed, you can say to this mountain,
move from here to there, and it will move.
Nothing will be impossible for you."*
—Jesus Christ, Matthew 17:20-21, Bible

* * * *

FAITH, SELF-CONFIDENCE, AND BELIEF are
extremely powerful forces. In fact, faith and belief are two
of the strongest messages that Jesus Christ and his disci-
ples preached to the needy. Many people know that Jesus
walked on water. But do you recall that Peter also walked on water
until his faith left him? It is vital to believe in yourself, other people, and most of all in the God who created you. Faith and belief are

vital to success and excellence. As Jesus said, "Everything is possible for him who believes" (Mark 9:23).

Without faith in yourself how can you hope to achieve your fullest potential? Watch how closely success in athletic performance follows the level of confidence of the athlete. *Lack of faith attracts failure like a magnet.* After dropping a ball or missing a shot an athlete may suddenly lose self-confidence, leading to a prolonged slump. Your attitude magnetizes you to success or failure. A positive self-image will pull positive things (and people) to you. Lack of self-confidence draws negative people and problems to you. It seems to be a law of nature.

So try to develop greater faith in yourself. Ralph Waldo Emerson said, "Self-trust is the first secret of success." You don't have to be an athlete to know the importance of self-confidence for high performance. A layoff, a missed promotion, or a family disappointment can slowly (or suddenly) cause you to lose belief in yourself. Try hard to catch yourself when this happens. Use self-talk, visualization skills, reflection, and prayer. You can't afford to lose faith in yourself because it is at the difficult times that you need it the most. Archbishop Desmond Tutu of South Africa stated in a recent TV commercial, "Of course, faith is risk, but one I would never risk living without."

Lack of faith attracts failure like a magnet.

Stay focused on the specific problem that confronts you and remind yourself of all the reasons you should be confident. When you get knocked down, you must get back up. As we said previously, be like a tennis ball. Football coaches often tell their players, "You will be judged not on whether you get knocked down, but on how fast you get up." Everyone gets knocked down, but don't let that knock you out. Be around positive and supportive people. Keep putting one foot in front of the other. Often the difference between winning and losing is just keeping at it. Confidence is a powerful force that will make you much more effective.

What have been some of your proudest accomplishments? Have you moved any mountains lately? Perhaps you have moved more than you realize. Have you helped someone at work to grow? Have you completed your education? Have you shown love to a child? Did you do something well at work? Have you supported your family in hard times? You have probably already moved many more mountains than you have realized. Reflect on your successes to build your confidence and belief in yourself. In fact, write them down NOW as you read this Pearl and keep them with you. With greater faith and self-confidence you can move larger mountains than you ever imagined.

Dr. Thurman Evans, a physician and motivational speaker, often shares with his audiences a story on faith about a little boy standing on a riverbank. An old man approaches him and says, "Young fellow, why are you just standing on the bank looking out?"

The little boy replied, "I am waiting for the big ship to come in."

The old man laughed and said, "Son, you are standing in the wrong place. See how the ships come in way down the other side of this river. You are in the wrong place." The little boy just stood there and said nothing. He started to smile and began rocking back and forth. The old man again said, "Little boy, you are standing in the wrong place." Just then a large ship appeared out of nowhere and stopped right in front of both of them. The old man looked at the ship and boy in amazement. Just then, a little boat was lowered from the big ship; men boarded the little boat and began rowing toward the boy. The little boat reached the riverbank, picked up the boy, and returned to the big ship. The boy was raised up from the little boat onto the ship.

Then the little boy looked out of the big ship and yelled to the old man: "You see, mister, I knew this ship would stop here because the captain of this ship is my daddy!" Do you have that type of faith? Your Father in heaven is always looking out for you. Trust in him. He knows the very number of hairs on your head. He knows every bird that falls in the forest and he knows (and values) you so much more. Read the Bible and you will see how much God cares. Trust in Him as this boy did with his father.

You must also believe in other people as well. You can't make it alone. There is a popular saying that goes, "Alone you can do it, but you can't do it alone." It is true that a few people can live in the wilderness or other places alone, but who wants to? Humans are social creatures. The better you function in a group, the better you function. To be successful you will need other people and you will need them to believe in you. Athletes must be able to believe in their teammates and in their coaching staff to be successful. If they don't come together and believe in each other as a team, they will stall like a car with bad timing. Notice that when great players reflect upon their individual achievements they always give credit to the other players and coaches who helped make it happen. This is not just being humble. It is being accurate. You need people out there block-ing for you. So look at your family and peers. Are they good? How can you improve them? Are the people you spend the most time with good people, loving people, and helpful people?

In his excellent book, *Think and Grow Rich*, Napoleon Hill describes the creation of a "mastermind group" to help people gen-erate ideas and grow wealthy together. Such a group of supportive people of a single mind (to help one another) can be extremely valu-able. Ideas can be bounced off each other, and the unique knowledge of someone else in the group may provide insight that you may have never realized. In addition, vital connections and friendships can be made. One member of the group may know someone else (not in the group) whose help could be vital to you.

Be careful to make only healthy relationships. Stay away from toxic people or at least limit your associations with them. As therapists we often hear sad stories of how poor choices in relationships lead to destruction of friendships, marriages, jobs, and families. Generally, it is wiser to make a mastermind group with people of your own gender. This helps keep people focused on the task at hand and avoids many potential problems. Also be careful of "wolves in sheep's clothing." These are people who do not truly have your interests in mind (even though they say they do). They follow the slick (but corrupting) advice of Marlon Brando's "Godfather": "Stay close to your friends, but stay closer to your enemies."

So search your heart and associate with the right people for the right reasons. You will need people a step or two ahead of you to provide the experience you lack. Likewise, you will need to help people not as far along as yourself. People on the right path make it a habit to help each other. If it is not practical to make a formal group, see or call people you respect for their advice. The road to success will be much smoother when you find help.

Have you ever driven in a HOV lane (the lane in big cities that requires at least two people in the car)?. Now think for a moment. Which were traveling faster, the cars in the HOV lane or the other cars? It's the cars in the HOV lane. Find help, and you will achieve your goals faster than if you go it alone. Think about it the next time someone passes you in the HOV lane.

We are not preachers and this is not a theological book. But our Christian faith is vitally important to us and we know that faith in God is your ultimate source of strength. The Bible is loaded with inspirational tales of faith. Included among them is the story of a woman being healed of her bleeding simply by touching the cloak of Jesus Christ, our Lord and Savior. In numerous examples throughout the New Testament, when Jesus healed the sick, he told them it was their *faith* that made them well. Clinical studies have repeatedly shown the importance of prayer and religious faith to mental health, physical health, and relationships. People may disappoint you, but God and Jesus Christ will not. Use spiritual faith to sort out your problems, plans, and dreams. In our experience the people with the greatest security, strength, and true joy are not the richest, biggest, prettiest, or most popular. They are people with the greatest faith in God. You will find greater belief in yourself through greater faith in the God who made you. Life is a gift, so make the most of it! God made you for a reason. Some people may approach you and say, "Who do you think you are? God's gift to the world?" You reply to them, "Yes I am." God wants you to be a gift to the world. Be your best in the truest sense of the word, defined by God's Word, and you will be content, successful, and happy.

* * * *

TRY THESE IDEAS:

1. Think about the mountains you have moved in your life. Write them down and take pleasure in them.

2. Develop an informal or formal mastermind group. Get together regularly or call them often.

3. Reflect on the faith you have in God. How might you strengthen this faith? Do you need to read the Bible more often, listen to spiritual books on tape, or go to church group? These are all your choices. Don't put them off for long.

* * * *

Suggested Affirmations: Say out loud 10 times, "I truly believe in my potential to be more than what I have been. I am in the HOV lane of success and am taking friends and family along with me."

* * * *

Write down the most important thing(s) to remember from this Pearl:

_____

_____

_____

_____

PEARL # 1 2

———— & ————

Remember the "Banana Theory"

*"'Know thyself,' said the old philosopher.
'Improve thyself,' said the new. Our great object
in time is not to waste our passions and gifts on
the things external that we must leave behind."*
—Edward George Bulwer-Lytton

* * * *

HAVE YOU EVER finally gotten around to throwing (or giving) away a bunch of old clothes and other junk in your attic, garage, or closet? It felt good to clean up, didn't it? That is what you must do with mental trash as well. Striving towards excellence does not mean simply taking on more mental "stuff," but also letting go of things you don't need.

Happiness and success often require getting rid of stuff. There's a story called "Operation Toss Away." In this story a man was a loner who never got involved with other people. He didn't date or social-ize. Instead, he got into a rut of just working everyday and watching TV after work. That's all he did. He was in a rut and didn't even

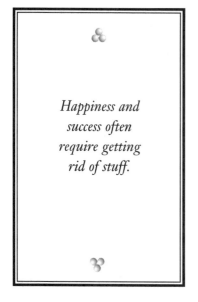

Happiness and success often require getting rid of stuff.

realize it. People didn't get close to him because he was distant and aloof. His problem was that he was carrying around an emotional load that was too heavy for him to carry alone. His mother had been an alcoholic and neglected him. His father had left when he was very young. He greatly resented his parents and let that regret impact every area of his life. Finally, a friend told him to get some help. Guess what happened when a therapist made him aware of these issues? He started letting go of his disappointments and anger; he worked on a better way to deal with his problems. He started to go to church and make a few new friends. In the end, how did he feel? He felt better—a lot better and a lot lighter. Letting go of emotional baggage is vital.

People often carry around psychological burdens and unnecessary mental baggage. They may not even be aware of all of the baggage because they've been doing it for so long! When you get rid of your mental baggage your mind can feel free again and your body will suddenly feel stronger and more energized! You will feel calmer and more content. What is your mental baggage? Is it a mother or father who disappointed you? Is it the job that got away, or a wrong turn in your life that you regret (over and over again)? The point is, if you can get rid of some of the old mental baggage, you can reduce a lot stress in your life. Reducing stress can improve your health and relationships and give you more energy for achieving success. If you can get rid of psychological baggage, you can be happier and more successful. Feelings such as anger, guilt, shame, and fear develop from mental baggage. These destructive emotions will stalk you, and given the chance, they'll tear at you like a rabid dog. Many causes of anger and despair are long gone and well beyond your control now. You must rid yourself of destructive feelings because they hold you back. Try your best to forgive. Jesus Christ said, "For if you forgive men when they sin against you, your Heavenly Father will also forgive you" (Matthew 6:14).

How do you get rid of toxic thoughts? You do that by DECIDING what your mind dwells on. If you find your thoughts starting down an old destructive path, stop and say to yourself: "No…I'm not going there today." You might also say "Delete, delete." You might replace a destructive thought with a positive one. You have far more control of your thoughts than you may have realized. Think for a moment. Weren't there times when you were tempted to do something or think something that was very wrong? You were able to resist (if you chose to) by controlling your thoughts, weren't you? The Bible teaches that God gives you no temptation beyond your control. It also teaches that He will always give you a way out from temptation. You can decide to go a different direction. You decide if you are going to think about old regrets, inappropriate thoughts, or frustrations. You decide if you are going to think about your blessings, family, and friends. The more often you "let go" or say "no" to destructive thoughts, the easier it will get. It really is that simple. Just decide that you will not let your thoughts linger on negative areas and it will become an easier and easier habit.

There's a well-known concept called the "Banana Theory." The "Banana Theory" refers to how monkeys were captured in certain parts of the world. Hunters would set a bamboo cage out in the jungle and put a banana inside the cage. The bars of the cage were just wide enough for the monkey to put its hand inside, but if the monkey grabbed a banana, it couldn't remove its hand. You get the idea. They would capture these monkeys because the monkeys would hold on to the bananas all day long and not let go! Think for a moment: how many people are like those monkeys, caught holding

Everyone has a few bananas they need to let go.

onto something that is causing danger, stress, and frustrations. All people have to do is "let it go." What the monkeys did doesn't make sense, does it? Think about those monkeys the next time you are wrestling with guilt, resentment, fear, anger, or some other emotion that pulls you down. Try to let go of your destructive emotions if you want to be successful.

Everyone has a few bananas they need to let go. It is important to recognize which bananas you are holding on to and then *decide to let them go.* However, we are not advocating the "easy way out" of simply "letting go" if you are having problems at school, in your marriage, or at work. Don't tell your wife or husband tonight that this Pearl has compelled you to get rid of some things in your life—and that he or she is number one on the list! Instead, we want you to let go of the destructive parts of your life, not those areas that are vulnerable and need more work and nourishment. It usually means deciding to let go of the fear, anger, guilt, selfish behaviors, insecurities, resentments, and toxic relationships. You decide if you will dwell on these things or not. You may need to *forgive* someone. You may need to forgive your parents, your spouse, your children, your boss, or perhaps yourself. Forgiving is a vital part of letting go. So try to control your emotions, or they will control you. Your thoughts and your emotions are yours. Decide to take control of them!

* * * *

TRY THESE IDEAS:

1. What guilt do you need to shed? Write it down, tear up the paper and forgive yourself.

2. Who are you angry at? Is this anger helping you or them? Let this go too.

3. What other "bananas" do you have to let go of? The sooner you decide to let go, the better.

* * * *

Suggested Affirmation: Say out loud 10 times, "I am letting go of the physical clutter in my closet, my toxic social relationships, and my mental clutter. Clutter has drained my energy in the past, but no more."

* * * *

Write down the most important thing(s) to remember from this Pearl:

_____

_____

_____

_____

PEARL #13

Limit Your Time With Toxic People

"Do not be misled: Bad company corrupts good character."
—Paul, 1 Corinthians 15:33, Bible

"Better a thousand enemies outside the house than one inside."
—Arabic proverb

* * * *

S A PHYSICIAN AND ADDICTION SPECIALIST, Dr. Hubbard often has to medically detoxify chemically-dependent people from addicting drugs such as alcohol, narcotics, benzodiazepines, and others. Detoxification is the first step before progress can occur towards a more rewarding life and rehabilitation. *We suggest that you detoxify yourself from the toxic people in your life!* Do you know who they are? They are the people who are poisonous to your goals, health, and spirit. They are the people at your work, social events, and neighborhood who make you feel unsafe, uneasy, and/or insignificant. They make you

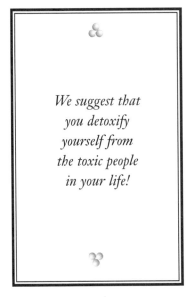

We suggest that you detoxify yourself from the toxic people in your life!

feel (actually you allow them to make you feel) drained of energy and demoralized. They are the people who bring you candy when you are on a diet or tell jokes at your expense. They are the people who prod you into inappropriate behaviors. You need to get rid of the toxic people in your life just as some people must rid themselves of toxic substances. If you can't completely get rid of certain toxic people, at least limit your time with them as much as possible.

Do not confuse toxic people from shy or socially lacking people. Some of these people may be really nice once you break through a few barriers. Toxic people, on the other hand, tell you why you won't be able to do something or why your ideas are stupid. Be sure your "friends" are your friends. Being a toxic person yourself is worse for you than being around toxic people. Being toxic to other people is destructive to your mind, relationships, and spirit. People are meant to help people, not hinder them.

What do toxic people want from you? They may want your time, money, car, energy, and/or your self-respect. They want from you whatever you have that they don't. They are entitled to whatever they can steal. Some may be "nice" to you in many ways, but very toxic and corrupting in others. All too often these days, there are self-centered people who may even want your husband or wife. Marriage means nothing to some toxic people. They don't care about their commitments and they certainly don't care about yours. They will entice anyone they are attracted to, whether the object of their flirtations is married or not. They can be dangerous to be around. At work they may tell your boss things that could cost you a promotion or even your job. We are not suggesting that you become paranoid. Rather, we want you to be smart. We think it is important that you recognize toxic people for who they are, and try to stay away from them!

Perhaps you are thinking you could help a particular toxic person. If you wish to exert a positive influence over such a person, then good for you; you might be able to help them. But be careful! Don't invest too much time or emotional energy in it. Look around and you will see that most of the time it is the toxic person who has the greater impact on people. Why is that? It is because toxic people don't play fair! Some lie, steal, cheat, seduce, and mislead. This is particularly true with children who are trying to fit in. A child trying to please a toxic person may get into drugs, expelled from school, or even become pregnant. Excepting those times when a toxic person has a particular problem you can specifically help with, try to stay in good company. As Paul said (Romans 16:17), "I urge you, brothers, to watch out for those who cause divisions and put obstacles in your way ... Keep away from them." If you want to help toxic people, *be a good example! Being a good example puts you at no risk and can help those who want to be helped.*

Try a technique called "creative neglect" with toxic people who do not want to change. It is a good way to get rid of toxic people. Let's say there is a man named Richard who is toxic to you. Perhaps he is a backstabber at work and wants your job. He tells you one thing and your boss another. The creative neglect technique employs various ways to stay away from him and neglect him as

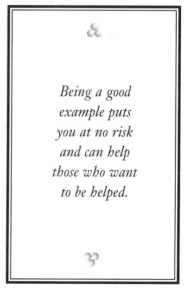

Being a good example puts you at no risk and can help those who want to be helped.

best you can. Have little or nothing to do with him (or her). We don't suggest you go out of your way to be rude. You should be as polite as you can; just try to minimize your time with that person. When he calls you up, say you are too busy to speak for more than a moment. When he wants to go somewhere with you, tell him you already have plans. If he continues to call you, just excuse yourself and hang up as quickly as possible. Eventually people like Richard will leave you alone.

If you think that creative neglect is not a nice thing to do, think about all the damage that can happen if the toxic person doesn't go away. Who will be hurt? It may be you, it may be your job, or it may be your family. After all, many people end up hurt if you get fired, swindled, or seduced into an inappropriate relationship. Did you know some difficult people are professionals at it? They are! While you and I are sleeping at night they are going to "difficult school," trying to learn how to be difficult. They must be, because they are so good at it!

Here are a couple more ideas about dealing with difficult people. Stop taking what they say and do so seriously. They are easier to neglect if you do not take them seriously. In fact, part of their problem may be the fun they derive from upsetting you. Consider learning a new set of skills. As Roger Mellot says (in his tape series, "Stress Management for Professionals"), "People should use *jerk skills* with toxic people as a way to neutralize them." Yes, you need to learn jerk skills. You have to become as efficient in your jerk skills as toxic people are efficient at being difficult. If you are a jerk to them, they may not wish to be around you. *Coping With Difficult People*, by Robert Bramson, is a great book on this topic. In fact, it's great in more ways than one: not only is its content useful, but the book *itself* is a valuable physical prop. Carry it around with you. Leave it on top of your desk. Let your difficult person see it each time he walks into your office. (Be creative with this one.)

Another good technique advocated by Roger Mellot is to remain calm and neutral when confronted by difficult people. This helps you stay in control of your emotions and will prevent those people from getting you upset. Toxic people like to catch you off guard: "Why didn't you do this thing or that?" What you need is a measured response: "I'm sorry I didn't finish it. I'll get it done." Try not to let them get you into a prolonged discussion or get your stress level up. Get NEUTRAL. When you let them upset you, you are giving them power over you. If you're lucky, you might even become too boring for them to be around you.

Have you heard of the old "bathroom technique"? When someone tries to trip you up, just say, "Excuse me for a moment, I need to go to the bathroom." This is a good one for people who are very dominating over you. While in the bathroom, take a few minutes to calm down, analyze the situation, and think. Learn stalling techniques (no pun intended) to deal with these people. Tell them you will indeed consider this or that, or that you'll get back to them later. Later on you can leave a brief note, send a short e-mail, or just completely forget about it. These people may be toxic, but they are often smart, pushy, and overbearing.

> [**A disclaimer for married readers:** Never try the bathroom technique at home! Why not? Because your husband or wife will simply follow you into the bathroom!]

Are you allowing a toxic person to rob you of your creativity, energy, self-esteem, or happiness? Take responsibility to rid yourself of toxic people so that you can grow faster and have more happiness. Toxic people are dangerous to your mind, body, and spirit.

* * * *

TRY THESE IDEAS:

1. Identify the people who are toxic to you. How can you avoid them?

2. Are you toxic to anyone? How can you change your behavior towards them?

3. Don't walk away from toxic people, run.

* * * *

Suggested Affirmation: Say out loud 10 times, "I am growing faster by freeing my life from toxic people."

* * * *

Write down the most important thing(s) to remember from this Pearl:

_____

_____

_____

_____

PEARL #14

&

Say No to Excessive Worry

*"Worry is a futile thing, it's somewhat like a rocking chair.
Although it keeps you occupied, it doesn't get you anywhere."*
—Anonymous

"Worry doesn't help anything, but it hurts everything."
—General George Patton

*"In my life time I've experienced many terrible things, only a
few of which actually happened."*
—Mark Twain

* * * *

WORRY IS A PART OF EVERYONE'S LIFE, but chronic worry can be a problem in and of itself. Do you find yourself worrying too much? Worry has become a regular pastime for many people. Excessive worry drains your energy and enthusiasm and can harm your health. It disrupts sleep and puts wear and tear on your mind and body. Pathological worry hinders relationships and ham-

If it festers, worry can grow like a cancer, disabling your ability to be successful.

pers your problem-solving ability. Worry does all these things to you and gives little back. *If it festers, worry can grow like a cancer, disabling your ability to be successful.*

Worry can initially be helpful. Like pain, worry serves the useful purpose of drawing your attention to a problem. Worry can motivate you to take important *action*. For example, if a man or woman has a heart attack, they have every reason to worry. That worry, however, should not lie dormant, but instead push the person into action. What action? They should examine their diet, level of exercise, how much they work, how much love they give and receive, and so on. And after that? The worrying should subside, because the person knows he or she is doing all they can. But if that person didn't take the appropriate actions, what would happen? They will worry and worry and worry...usually until they have another heart attack. Doing all you can do always gives you greater peace. Then you must try to "let go and let GOD." If it continues for long, worry becomes a problem unto itself. It may even lead to feelings of fear, paranoia, and/or depression, which cause even more misery.

Not only can worry worsen your ability to correct a problem, but most worries never even come true! As Thomas Jefferson said, "How much pain they have cost us, the evils which have never happened." All the pain of worrying is wasted when the worry never materializes. The "what if" worry is a very common one. "What if my boss doesn't like this report?" "What if I lose my job?" "What if I lose my boyfriend?" "What if?"..."What if?" People suffer endlessly from "what if" worry, often for nothing.

If you cannot stop excessive worry, try doing it during a pre-planned "worry time" each day. Take 15–30 minutes every day to just sit and worry. During your pre-planned "worry time" or "reflection time" you can worry and worry until you are totally worried out. Use this time to worry about today's ups and downs and what problems you expect tomorrow. Try to use this time to let out your fears and explore them for what they are. What are the real chances that your worry will come true? What can you do if it does occur?

This is an especially good idea for those of you who have trouble sleeping, because many people don't begin to think about their day and the one to come until they lay their head down on the pillow! If you have problems sleeping, here is another good suggestion. Don't keep checking your clock. You are not going anywhere. This habit only keeps you frustrated and awake, fretting over the sleep you've lost and the sleep you still need. Sleeping problems then compound whatever is causing your worries!

So have a worry time and write down solutions to problems as you think of them, rather than rehashing them throughout the day. Use your visualization techniques to turn worry into constructive ideas and plans. Use prayer and your affirmations to give you strength.

Think about this often told Chinese fable. A poor Chinese man had one son and a horse. One day his horse got out of the stable and ran away. Is that good or bad? Two weeks later, the horse came back with 20 stallions. Is that good or bad? Sounds good, but it could be

> &
>
> *So have a worry time and write down solutions to problems as you think of them, rather than rehashing them throughout the day.*
>
> ⅋

bad because he had to feed those 20 stallions. One day his son tried to ride one of the horses, fell, and broke his leg. Is that good or bad? Two weeks later the Chinese army came to draft this young man to fight in a war far away. They couldn't draft him because he had a broken leg. Is that good or bad? (This story has no real ending, does it?) The point of the fable is to try and take life in stride. You may be worrying about things now that will lead to a better ending than you ever imagined.

Many things are good or bad depending how you look at them. And often what you think is bad at a certain time in your life turns out to be good in the long run. Losing an existing job may result in obtaining an even better job. Erwin Hubbard (Dr. Hubbard's father), for example, was stuck at a particular job for over thirty years because he didn't want to risk taking a new job and putting his large family in financial jeopardy. Then, when his company went belly-up, he was out of work for months. He kept his cool and eventually landed a new job with a smaller company. Although he did not start out at the top, in just a few years he became Vice President of Finance and was making more money than he ever dreamed. You don't have to look hard to find other people with similar stories.

In another example, a woman was depressed because her husband divorced her after many years of marriage. He had had multiple affairs and eventually felt the need to marry one of his other women. Though blameless, his wife was nonetheless upset and thought her life was over. But guess what? A few years later she found someone else who was faithful and cared about her much more than her first husband ever did. Of course, we are not advocating divorce. But this woman had no choice in the matter and benefited from a situation that had seemed disastrous.

Having problems in your life means you are alive. There may be a gift in there somewhere. Make the most of whatever change comes your way, whether you planned the change or not. In some cases resolution of a problem (such as illness) may make you more thankful for what you have. What can being positive hurt? Could being positive help? You bet it can, and it does.

Have you had times that seemed too dark to get through and yet things ended up well? It happens to all of us. Winston Churchill stated, "A pessimist sees the difficulties in every opportunity; an optimist sees the opportunities in every difficulty." How many times have you gone down a certain road in life (such as a new job) and been forced to take a detour, only to discover that the new path was even better? Remind yourself that the road you previously traveled probably had its own difficulties. In fact, it might have been fraught with future problems you couldn't even imagine—by changing roads, you avoid these would-be obstacles. As Norman Vincent Peale said, "Always interpret things happening to you in a positive way." Find the positives because it brings more positives into your life. It allows you to be content and happy. Some people may say it is absurd to try and find the positive during problems. We think it is absurd *not* to!

Remember, you are a survivor. As Iyanla Vanzant (a lawyer and best-selling author) said, "Stop focusing upon what is happening to you, but more on how you are getting through what happens to you." You have had hard times before and survived them. You will again. Say to yourself, "I have survived worse than this, I'll be okay." Ask yourself what you can learn from your experience? Ask yourself if you are growing in a positive direction. Rid your thinking of the "would have beens," "should have beens," and "could have beens." These thoughts are called "stinkin thinkin" in the substance abuse field because they hold people back. Negative attitudes act as anchors in your life and in your relationships. You will survive! You may even prosper from your current problems in ways you cannot even imagine! Perhaps you will land a better job or perhaps you will grow closer to God in times of hardship. Stay positive. Positive thinking attracts positive results like a magnet!

For some people, chronic worry may be so bad that professional help is needed. If so, find that help. Some of the new antidepressants have wonderful anti-anxiety properties to treat what is called "Generalized Anxiety Disorder" (GAD). GAD is in fact just one of many clinical anxiety disorders that go beyond normal anxiety. Obsessive-compulsive disorder—where people do things over and over for no reason (such as excessive checking, counting, hand washing, or cleaning)—is another anxiety-related disorder that can be very debilitating. Other people have uncontrollable panic attacks or very severe phobias. You may want to consult your general doctor or a psychiatrist if you think your worry or anxiety problem is excessive and cannot be controlled. Dr. Hubbard is a psychiatrist who has witnessed the great benefits of these medications combined with therapy. But whether or not one is taking medication, everyone can benefit by putting into action our psychological approaches towards reducing worry.

* * * *

TRY THESE IDEAS:

1. Write down your three biggest worries. Decide how to turn worry into ordinary concerns. Make plans to handle your big problems.

2. Develop a "worry time" so that the rest of the time you don't have to worry.

3. Think of two or three worries in your life that never came true. How much did you suffer for these things that never happened?

4. Think about how a person who you admire would look at the same situation and solve your problem.

* * * *

Suggested Affirmations: Say out loud 10 times, "I am only focusing upon good things that might happen to me."

* * * *

Write down the most important thing(s) to remember from this Pearl:

_____

_____

_____

_____

PEARL #15

&

Be Employable

*"There is only a little difference between people,
but a little difference makes a big difference."*
—*W. Clement Stone's "Slight Edge Principle"*

"The future is for the competent."
—*Brian Tracy*

"I believe that everyone lives by selling something."
—*Robert Louis Stevenson*

* * * *

IT IS BELIEVED THAT MOST PEOPLE use only about 10% of their brains and thus never optimize their full ability level. Did you know that? Have you ever wondered what happened to the other 90%? Think about this: If you just increased your brain power from 10% to 20%, you'd be a success. We are not asking you to go from 10% to 80%, or from 10% to 50%. Just from 10% to 20%. Increase that much and you'd be a huge success! You will at least double your output. We say "at least" because when people succeed they create a positive momentum which, in turn, often sets off a rapid chain reaction of accomplishments. Isn't it good to know that there is much more potential in you than you had ever dreamed? The trick is to get the most from yourself.

Despite the ups and downs of our economy and the fact that all companies are in some type of transition, making a good living in the USA is not as hard as in most other places in the world. Most Americans were born with a head start on people from other countries. Being a U.S. citizen is like being a Roman in ancient times. It is a great advantage because the U.S. is the most powerful economic and military nation in the world. Earl once spoke with the CEO of a large, South African company and the two compared their countries. The difference between South Africa and the USA, the CEO pointed out, is that when an American loses his job, he or she often needs only walk across the street and find another one. But in South Africa if a person loses their job, they may *never* get another job!

Some studies indicate that before they retire, today's new workers in the U.S. will have twenty-five jobs and five to six career changes. What this means is that employers will be looking for versatile, self-managed, easily trained, confident employees who can get the job done in an ever changing work environment.

*Being employed empowers the employer over you. But being **employable** empowers **you**!*

It's often said: "Don't just work on being employed, work on being employable." *Being employed empowers the employer over you. But being **employable** empowers **you**!* There's a big difference, isn't there? The feeling of empowerment can make a huge difference in your confidence, opportunities, and happiness. It creates an "I'm on a mission" attitude within you.

Be an employable person by developing your knowledge and talents in your chosen field. Keep studying and developing new skills. If for some reason your company downsizes, you will have far less to worry about than the person who was lucky just to have been there. Your employers should be lucky to have you! Be an employable person who is constantly working on yourself. It will also help you develop survival skills in a world that is constantly changing.

The days of companies rewarding your mere loyalty with guaranteed employment are *long gone*. Just look around and notice what has happened to those who thought, "This company is like my family. They will take care of me like my mother did." Wake up! No company today will ever be your mother. So stop saying, "It's not in my job description." Start attempting new projects, start taking time to ask for help, and start doing whatever it takes to find a mentor who will help teach you to get ahead.

If you studied journals, books, and other sources of information in your field for just a little while every day, you would soon be well ahead of your peers. The fact is, once they land a job, most people relax; they abandon their learning efforts. You will have an advantage if you continually further your formal and informal education in ways that make you a better employee. Develop better communication skills. Communication skills are vital for almost every job and can be the key to rapid advancement. People with good communication skills can not only find jobs easier, but often rise more quickly to the top. Consider enhancing your computer skills. Computers are here to stay. The more you know about computers the greater the advantage you will have in many fields. Go to seminars, read books, and find mentors in areas you need to improve. Make yourself valuable. If for some reason your company cuts back, you will not have to look far to find another job.

Many good hard-working people stay stuck at a job far below their potential because they work harder on their job than on themselves. Let's take a look at two women. Judy is a young worker who is employed as a computer programmer. When the boss says to make a certain program, she does it. In between those times she hides out in the lunchroom or at her desk playing computer games and e-mailing friends. After work she goes home, has a couple beers, and watches TV until bedtime. Know anyone like that? Now, Elaine is also a young computer programmer with the same company. She also develops programs when she is asked to do so by her boss. At lunch, she often sits with more senior people in the company and asks them questions. Elaine finds out more about the company and how other people advanced there. At night she takes courses in business administration and advanced computer programming. Guess who will climb the corporate ladder more quickly or become a supervisor in a couple of years? Judy works hard at her job, but Elaine works hard on *herself* (as well as her job). Be employable. Most employers will be happy to see you develop new skills because you will be more useful to them.

All of the Pearls presented in this book will help you become more employable if you put them into practice. Take a look at the other Pearls. You can develop great habits from them. Would you want to hire someone who used these Pearls at work and in other areas of their life? We would!

* * * *

TRY THESE IDEAS:

1. Write down three ways to make you more employable. Make a plan to get them into action.

2. Evaluate your weaknesses in your field. How might you strengthen them?

* * * *

Suggested Affirmation: Say out loud ten times, "I am an entrepreneur adding value to my job, myself, my family, and my community."

* * * *

Write down the most important thing(s) to remember from this Pearl:

P E A R L # 1 6

Consider the Narrow Path

"Find out what most people do and don't do it."
—Jim Rohn

*"Enter through the narrow gate. For wide is the gate
and road that lead to destruction...But small is the
gate and narrow the road that leads to life,
and only a few find it."*
—Jesus Christ, Matthew 7:13-14, Bible

*"If you are hard on yourself, life will be easy;
if you are easy on yourself, life will be hard."*
—Zig Ziglar

* * * *

ARE YOU SEARCHING FOR SOMETHING to do with your life? Are you looking for a way to earn more money or make a difference? Try what motivational speaker Jim Rohn and others have suggested: study what other people are doing, and do something different. Do something

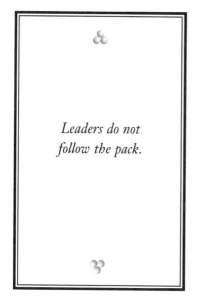

Leaders do not follow the pack.

unique. If everyone else is providing a certain service, why do they need you to do the same thing? *Leaders do not follow the pack.* You know what they say, those who follow are always looking at someone else's hind end. Doing what other people are NOT doing may be what puts you ahead of the game, rather than being a step behind. Of course, some ideas are just plain bad and are not pursued because they clearly will not work. But many novel ideas never come to fruition simply because they are never tried. In other cases, half-hearted attempts or attempts at the wrong time or wrong place may have scared people away from a potentially rewarding area. Be creative and be smart. Do your homework. As we say in another Pearl, don't just take risks, take smart risks.

If you want to succeed quickly, find out what people really need but are not getting. We suggest you try asking them. Yes, literally *ask* them. In fact, this basic approach of asking is being successfully used by more and more political campaigns. These "focused groups" (as they are called) tell politicians what people are thinking. You can follow their example by asking questions like, "What are you looking for?" "What do you want?" "What would you like to have in your community, home, or work that you don't have now?" Ask a lot of people in your community. Are you getting the same response, again and again? It could be that a reliable auto garage or computer repair service is needed in your area. Perhaps it is a hardware store or a laundromat that people ask for. Day-care, cleaning services, landscaping—who knows? The answer will differ from location to location. And a "wrong" answer five years ago may be the right option now. But if you can provide what is truly needed or truly wanted in your area, what a success you will be!

A good example is demonstrated by Dr. Hubbard's friend, a doctor who ran a successful practice, specialized in the treatment of a particular illness. His success, however, didn't stop him from reaching out to community groups and asking what *else* his field could offer. The ensuing feedback resulted in the development of a new clinician group to provide the complex combination of services that was truly needed in the community. The mutual reward was greater income for the doctors and better care for the patients. As Dr. Hubbard's friend puts it, "We are kicking ass. No other group in the community can compete with us." By asking people want they need, he discovered a new path towards increased success, all the while continuing to do what he loves.

See the world around you for what it is (not what you want it to be) and try to find a special niche for yourself. Look around at your current place of employment. In what area is your company lacking? Is there a need for improvement in marketing approaches, teamwork, innovation, or perhaps leadership? Can you help to fill a particular gap at your work? Finding a need at work and filling that need will make you that much more valuable. Fortunes have been made on just one simple idea being put into action. That is, if the world (or a small part of it) stood to benefit from that simple idea.

Consider the well-known concept of "marketing" verses "operational" thinking. Operational processes give people what they

> *See the world around you for what it is (not what you want it to be) and try to find a special niche for yourself.*

expect. If you go to a motel for a nice, clean room, you get one. Marketing processes also give the customer a nice, clean room, but they give even more without being asked! They may put mints on the pillows, flowers on the desk, or provide a free breakfast. Marketing approaches give more so that the people they serve remember them. Marketing thinkers take the narrow path. They do the unexpected and give more to get more. Best-selling author Zig Ziglar is considered by many to be the world's foremost motivational speaker. He has said, "If you do more than what you are paid to do, you will eventually get paid more than what you do." Ask yourself, "Am I doing more than what is asked from me to do my job?"

So take a close look at what people are doing, and what people aren't doing. Consider the narrow path. How can your talents lead to providing a needed service or product? How can you become more valuable at work? Often this is a difficult question to answer. But if you answer this question well, the possibilities are enormous, and the rewards can be great. And don't leave this approach at work. Ask yourself, "How can I become a better, very special parent or spouse?" Success at home is what really makes life more beautiful.

It may take some time to sort through various ideas to find one that excites you. Do your homework well. Be patient, but be determined and insightful.

* * * *

TRY THESE IDEAS:

1. What does your work need? Can you provide it? If so, your value in the company will be greatly enhanced.

2. What does your family need? See if you can help more in that area. If you don't know what your family member needs from you, simply ask them.

* * * *

Suggested Affirmation: Say out loud 10 times, "I am moving along the narrow path which is taking me where I want to go."

* * * *

Write down the most important thing(s) to remember from this Pearl:

_____

_____

_____

_____

PEARL # 17

Rid Yourself of Envy and Resentments

"To be wronged is nothing unless you continue to remember it." —**Confucius**

"Once a woman has forgiven her man, she must not reheat his sins for breakfast."
—**Marlene Dietrich**

* * * *

IF YOU WENT TO A PLAYGROUND and saw some small children suddenly break into a fight, what would happen after you broke it up? The odds are, the young children would be playing again within 5-10 minutes like it never happened. If that is what we call "child's play," then we need more of it. If two adults get into an argument they may not speak to each other again for 20 years! And that is adult behavior, isn't it? If a person is truly toxic to you (on a regular basis) then perhaps you don't need to speak or associate with them. However, too often good friends or family members have a problem that lingers on in resentment merely because they do not talk and work it out. Often there is merely a misunderstanding that needs to be clarified. In some cases an apology is all that is needed to cure the resentment. Life is too short to keep you from an old friend or family member.

Envy and resentment are common emotions, but ones that weigh you down. *People carry around envy and resentments like a heavy pack of rocks on their back.* Resentments hold you back and keep you from moving ahead. They allow others to have power over you. If you are constantly resentful of a person at work, it will affect both your performance on the job and your happiness. It allows them to continuously have a negative impact on you.

Where do envy and resentments start? They often start when people are very young. Perhaps you believed that some of your friends or neighbors had more toys, were more popular, or had a nicer house than you did growing up. Perhaps you resented the way some kids (or siblings) teased you. Maybe a teacher publicly humiliated you instead of enhancing your self-esteem. These old childhood hurts can be very tough to discard. They occur when people are immature; years later, people often continue to react in the same immature way. When people talk about their childhood emotional hurts they often regress before your eyes and become emotional about them all over again. This is normal. However, you need to stay on guard to prevent old hurts from causing you continued resentment and hindering your happiness now.

> &
>
> *People carry around envy and resentments like a heavy pack of rocks on their back.*

It seems to be human nature to look at the hundreds of people who "have it better" than yourself, while ignoring the millions who have it worse. That is really too bad, isn't it? Some people do have more money, are more popular, or have the loving family you desire. But you don't have to look very hard to find people who have it much, much worse than you! People don't like to look at sad things, so they tend to ignore slums, unpleasant areas, poor countries, and even sick or unattractive people. Even though it is

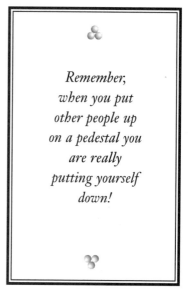

Remember, when you put other people up on a pedestal you are really putting yourself down!

human nature to admire and compare yourself with people who (you think) have it better, you must recognize the harm that it does to your heart and spirit if it leads to envy or resentment. *Remember, when you put other people up on a pedestal you are really putting yourself down!* In addition, ignoring those who need help also decreases the likelihood that you will have compassion for them and help when you can. Work harder to emulate (not resent) those you admire and assist those in need.

Do you envy people who have bigger houses, are more attractive, or drive fancier cars? If so, do you also worry about all those people who have smaller houses, are less attractive, and take the bus? A woman may compare herself to another woman's beauty while ignoring (or not knowing) that the other pretty woman has an abusive husband, is a cocaine addict, or suffers from cancer. A man may resent another man's prestigious job, but be unaware that the stress of it will give him a heart attack in one or two years. It is important to remember that envy and resentment are often based on ignorance of the whole story. If a person owns some possessions that are truly better than yours, then good for them! But you don't know everything about that person. Given the choice—*and* the whole story—you wouldn't necessarily switch places with that person.

When Earl read "Richard Cory" the poem by Edwin Arlington Robinson as a child it affected his perspective on life, and it still touches him today. The poem describes a man who appears to have everything. Both rich and handsome he is admired by all and many would leap to change places with him. The poem ends with Richard Cory putting a bullet in his head and no one knew why.

Perhaps your envy or resentment turns to anger towards your wife or husband because they haven't given you the things you feel you need. This is a common source of conflict and brings misery to many marriages. However, it is important to recognize that problems are often illusory; a more positive way of thinking will improve your outlook, and, in turn, your situation. For example, many housewives envy other women who are employed, while many employed women envy the housewives. It is the perception of things that often makes people envious, rather than reality. Always remember that a positive attitude and thankfulness will make you happier in any situation. It will also put your in a better place spiritually and emotionally.

It is interesting to note just how wrong perceptions can be. Stories emerge every day about how ex-athletes who were envied by millions of fans have become bankrupt, live with chronic pain, or endure drug problems. Other stories report music stars who make millions of dollars in album sales, but barely make a living after the lawyers, promoters, producers and countless assistants get their share. Movie stars have the world at their feet one week, and they get arrested for drugs and file for divorce the next. It seems that celebrities routinely end up in hurtful and broken relationships. Yet so many people continue to envy them because of their apparent beauty, talent, riches, and fame.

The fact is, you really don't know whom to envy! The person to admire most may not be the beautiful movie star on the cover of *People* magazine. It may be the quiet neighbor down the road with two jobs, a loving wife, and three beautiful children. It may be the alcoholic who has become sober and regained his life. Resentments only hold you back; they dampen your spirit, weaken your character, and do harm to others.

Where do your resentments lie? All resentments originate in your mind as a result of skewed thinking. And because they spring from your thoughts, it means you can control them. Is there a better way to view things? Can you leave resentments behind? Can you be more like a child in this area? Children forgive quickly and move on because they want to have fun. Holding onto resentment can affect what people think of you and impair your ability to be successful. Remember, resentments do nothing but harm you and keep you from being your best.

Remember, in the end it is not between you and them, but between you and the Lord.

* * * *

TRY THESE IDEAS:

1. Reflect on your envy or resentments at home and at work. Find a better approach to deal with them.

2. Forgive your parents, spouse, friends and colleagues. It will free you even more than them.

* * * *

Suggested Affirmation: Say out loud 10 times, "I am feeling lighter and lighter because I am no longer holding onto resentments."

* * * *

Write down the most important thing(s) to remember from this Pearl:

_____

_____

_____

_____

PEARL # 18

Courage and Smart Risk Taking

*"All our dreams can come true–if we have
the courage to pursue them."*
—Walt Disney

"The will to do, the soul to dare."
—Sir Walter Scott

*"The only way you will be able to move forward
is to accept mistakes as a part of life,
learn from them, and improve."*
—John Maxwell

"Life is a great adventure or nothing at all."
—Helen Keller

* * * *

&

Plain and simple, to be your best, you will need the courage to take a few smart risks.

ℬ

IF YOU WANT to have a better life and more opportunities, make more progress, open the gates to your dreams, sharpen your vision and focus, and truly separate yourself from the pack of society, then this Pearl is for you.

Plain and simple, to be your best, you will need the courage to take a few smart risks. Earl recalls attending a seminar by Robert Laser, an international expert consultant on negotiation in Atlanta. At the beginning of Robert's presentation, he asked for four audience volunteers to quickly come up to the front of the room. Everyone in the room was silent and didn't move. People started to look everywhere except at the front of the room. Some people looked down, some people looked around, and some prayed silently that someone else in the room would go up to the front. The tension intensified. Some started to scratch their heads. Amazingly, Earl noticed only three people go up. They did not know what to expect. When the three arrived in the front, Robert asked the audience to give them a big round of applause and asked them to take their seats again. The three were surprised and quite pleased with themselves. These three people were willing to risk the unknown. The point Robert Laser was making was that very few people are willing to take risks to succeed. People like to stay in their comfort zones and let opportunity come to them. You might be wondering what Earl did. He sat there! Yes, Earl sat there. Of course that was ten years ago, and he learned a valuable lesson that day. Now he puts other people on the spot, and rewards them well.

You cannot be your best if you never take risks. That is, if you always focus on your fears (i.e., the worst that can happen), it is unlikely that you will achieve your best. It is a risk to go to college, get a new job, or commit to marriage. You do not have a crystal ball to look perfectly into the future. Yet each of these endeavors can yield wonderful benefits. How can you get a better job without trying? How can you have a loving home life without committing to someone to share it with, according to the rules of God? Many adults have lost their courage to take chances in life. They like to play it safe and take no risk that can be avoided. They are the "what if" people. What if I go to college and fail? What if my marriage isn't wonderful forever? What if my new job ends up worse than the old one? If you want to be successful, you cannot base your life on the assumption that something may go wrong. After all, something may go terribly right! So steel yourself up and find the courage to take exciting (and appropriate) new actions.

Of course, we are not promoting recklessness. You should not take every risk that comes your way. *In fact, you may need to take only one or two smart risks in your life to do well.* The trick is to be a *smart* risk taker. Recklessness is not the path to success or excellence. People looking for trouble by taking unnecessary risks will always find it. True gamblers always lose in the long run; the odds are always with the house. (In general, gambling types don't seek personal growth; they are often immature and restless. Always looking for quick fixes, they are rarely satisfied.) Take risks with good odds of success, at the right time, and when your heart feels it is the right direction to go. Plans to

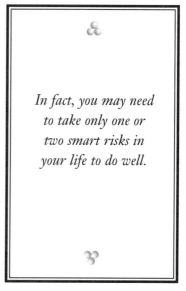

In fact, you may need to take only one or two smart risks in your life to do well.

fulfill your dreams are never fool-proof, but courage to take a few risks is almost always needed to make those dreams come true.

A major university did a four-year study on happiness. They asked what the key to happiness is. Can you guess what scored first in their study? It wasn't love. It was risk taking! The researchers found that people who were risk takers were happier than people who always stayed in their comfort zone, or their "box." People spend too much time their comfort zone. They don't realize that *not* taking risks is a risk too! That bears repeating: never taking a risk is perhaps the greatest risk of all! So why be overly cautious? A soldier may be shot advancing on the enemy, but he (or she) can also be shot running from the battle. Which wound do you think would hurt the most?

When a university study examined highly successful married couples, most of the respondents said, "We went through rough times to get to the good times." Getting through the bad times makes the good times all the more enjoyable. The problem with some people is that they expect all times to be good times. If you expect nothing but good times, you will experience considerable disappointment with your job, marriage, and other people. Risk taking may bring some bad with the good, but remember: bad times will happen anyway, no matter where you are or what direction you take.

If you have a dream to own your own business, how can it possibly succeed without the courage to get it started! Can you image the risks George Washington, Thomas Jefferson, Alexander Hamilton, Benjamin Franklin, and others took in the 1700's to form a new nation called the United States of America? The British Empire was the greatest power in the world. These men and other colonists could very well have been put to death if they did not succeed. These patriots were already wealthy and successful men, yet they felt that creating a new, free country was the right thing to do and worth risking everything for. Millions of other people in the U.S. have since been rewarded for the risks they took.

As a mother or father you must take some risks with your children in order to help them grow up. Letting them spend the night at a friend's house is a risk. Letting them play sports is a risk. But how will they grow otherwise? Being overprotective does not feel like a risk, but it is. You risk their resentment. You risk your child being left behind, unprepared, and ridiculed. You risk your child not getting the exercise they need or not feeling part of their peer group. Your children will be on their own one day. Have they been given enough freedom (and restraint) to be ready? As Helen Keller said, "Avoiding danger is no safer in the long run than outright exposure. The fearful are caught as often as the bold."

Where do YOU need to take a smart risk or two? Do you need to risk going back to school? What would be a smart risk to take at work? Do you need to risk asking for a raise or for more vacation time? These are questions that are important to ask yourself. You must take responsibility for the risks that you take, whether they work or not. Don't be reckless, but be aware that successful people all take a few risks to achieve their dreams. Take risks that build your character not ones that can destroy it.

Finally, we must warn you that you will make a mistake or two. Expect it; you are human. Growth often does not occur in a straight line. If you take a risk and it doesn't work out, do not panic. Regroup and sort out where things went wrong. Learn from the mistake. Do not crucify yourself or others when things don't go your way. Stay positive. Use the "TAP" method we discussed in the Mission Statement of this book to find your way out of the dilemma. Have faith that you can do it and don't let the bad experience put you in a box. If you fall off a horse, you have to get back on right away to keep fear from paralyzing you. Don't be afraid to take the next opportunity, if it is a *smart* risk. Have courage to do what is right.

* * * *

TRY THESE IDEAS:

1. In what areas do you need to show more courage at work? When do you need to avoid being reckless?

2. Think of the road ahead this year in other aspects of your life. Where do you need courage and faith?

* * * *

Suggested Affirmations: Say out loud 10 times, "I am becoming more successful than ever before because I am learning to have courage and faith to do the things that I should."

* * * *

Write down the most important thing(s) to remember from this Pearl:

_____

_____

_____

_____

PEARL # 19

Your Life Is More Than Your Job

"Learn to give yourself to yourself,
before you give yourself away."
—Susan Taylor

"Work harder on yourself than on your job."
—Jim Rohn

* * * *

WORKING HARD ON YOUR JOB is important, but working harder on yourself is a powerful idea that motivational speaker Jim Rohn and
others so wisely advocate. When people decide
to work harder, they generally think about increasing their effort on
their job. This is true whether their job is a corporate executive,
laborer, or homemaker. Many people, especially men, think that just
working hard on their job is all they need to do. Make no mistake,
your work is important. Employment supports you and your fami-

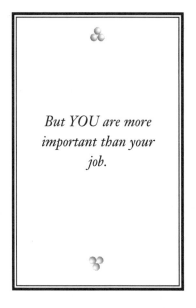

But YOU are more important than your job.

ly. Much of this book's content is designed to help you be more effective at work (and to help you enjoy your work). *But YOU are more important than your job.*

You cannot afford to put all your time and energy into work alone. If you put all your effort into your job you will have little time or energy for much else. Eventually, you will find that it leads to poor health, marital problems, neglected children, and estranged friends and neighbors. There have been countless salesman, doctors, lawyers, businessmen, nurses, politicians, and others who have found out too late that their dedication to their job was excessive and that it eventually brought pain to their families and to themselves. Rabbi Kersner talks about this in his book, *When All You Ever Wanted Is Not Enough*. The rabbi reflects on working with dying patients. As he watched them die, not one of them said, "I wish I had spent more time at the office." Almost all of them proclaimed, "I wish I had spent more time with my family." Providing for your family is more than a paycheck. Working on your life means greater balance in the multiple areas of your life. The reflection Pearl earlier in this book hopefully got you headed in that direction already.

There are many stories that relate to this issue. One man we heard about was in the armed service. He and his wife saved their money and sacrificed for nearly thirty years. When he retired as a lieutenant colonel they had a lot of money saved because they had sacrificed so much for so long. The sad part of the story, however, is that she died of cancer a year later. She never reaped the rewards of their sacrifice. He had worked so hard in the military service that not only was he left alone, but he did not know what to do outside of work. He became unhappy. He is still trying to find himself. Many policemen, doctors, corporate executives, and firemen are also often reported to be lost souls after they retire if they did not have balance in their lives beforehand.

Every place of employment is different. The people are different, attitudes are different, the working environment is different, and expectations can be quite different. Some work environments are supportive and some are not. It is up to you to determine if your employer's demands have thrown your life out of balance or if the job is right for you. Evaluate and re-evaluate your situation. Sometimes things change. If necessary, can you discuss the problem with your boss or employee representatives to get your life back on track? Your employer may be more understanding than you realize. He or she is, after all, only a person too. Your boss may relate very easily to your concerns. You may find out that it was not your employer overworking you after all, but YOU who was overworking you. You may feel frantic and overwhelmed as a result of all the overtime you've been taking on. But you can't blame your employer for that. They merely offered the overtime. *You* accepted it. It is in everyone's best interest for you to be a great worker, but under conditions that also make you a great person, both at work and at home.

At home there are many mothers who are so dedicated to their children that they too often neglect themselves and their marriages. They stop exercising, doing things they enjoy, and doing things with their husbands. They put every ounce of energy into their children. This imbalance can lead to marital discord and health problems and ultimately threaten the happiness and cohesion of the family. It will also affect the children. Neglected husbands or wives may become irritable and isolate themselves; even worse, they may start drinking or keep other types of inappropriate company. Doctors and therapists hear these stories in their clinics everyday. Parents

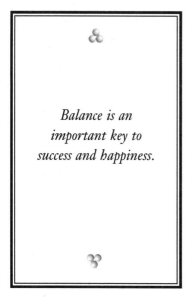

Balance is an important key to success and happiness.

must remember that children would rather see their parents be happy and together than have more toys or more pampering. Love and care for your children are vital. But care for yourself and your spouse is vital as well.

So remember, work is important, but you need to work on yourself more. You are a child of God and you deserve it. In fact, this is the major reason you are reading this book isn't it? Do you need to work on your health, love life, spiritual life, or relationship with your children? *Balance is an important key to success and happiness.* The better you are, the better you will be on your job.

Are you working consistently on your self-development? Are you exercising, sleeping enough, reading, learning new skills, and developing relationships? Are you nurturing your spouse, children, and yourself? Is the best of you coming home at night or are you leaving it at work? Too many people "rise to the occasion" at work but not at home. Too often people think it should be "easy" at home. But guess what. Home life takes effort too, but the rewards of love and contentment are greater than anything your job has to offer. Personal growth is the best thing you can do for yourself, your job, your community, and most important, your family.

* * * *

TRY THESE IDEAS:

1. Decide on one or two self-development ideas to have a healthier body. Do you need to walk? Do you need to join a gym?

2. Decide on a self-development idea to make you more valuable at work. Do you meet to learn a new skill? Do you need to make more connections?

3. Decide how you can be more valuable to your husband or wife. A happy spouse will make a happier you.

* * * *

Suggested Affirmation: Say out loud 10 times, "I am putting myself and my family first. As a result, I am bringing more value to my job."

* * * *

Write down the most important thing(s) to remember from this Pearl:

_____

_____

_____

_____

PEARL # 20

Whining Does Not Lead to Winning

"We have first raised dust and then complain we cannot see."
—Bishop Berekeley

"Without struggle there is no progress."
—Frederick Douglass

"I never saw a wild thing sorry for itself. A small bird will drop frozen dead from a bough without ever having felt sorry for itself."
—D.H. Lawrence

"Whining does not equal winning — misery is an option."
—seen on a bumper sticker

* * * *

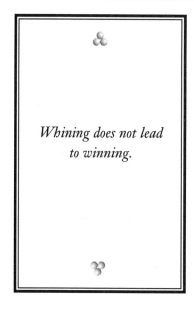

Whining does not lead to winning.

Whining does not lead to winning. Do you like to be around whiners, or do you like to be with winners? You know who the whiners are. They are the ones who never think things are good enough. They complain about their job, their spouse, their boss, and their children. Their vacation was not good enough or long enough. Even while on vacation and sitting on the beach, they will complain about the weather. Their husband does not make enough money or their wife isn't affectionate enough, or vice versa. Whiners think that by complaining they may get an easier job, more money, or new friends.

If you observe them closely you will find that whiners hang around other whiners. Have you ever seen a whiner's club at your office? Whiners may get their way now and then, but they never get very far. They win a battle here and there, but they never win the war. The friends they make will soon be complainers too (if they aren't already). Can you imagine the fun they have complaining about their jobs, the boss, the economy, their spouse and who knows what else? Isn't it a shame when one whiner teaches someone else how to be like them?

Whiners are people who characteristically think only of themselves. While one whiner is complaining, the others aren't listening as much as they are reflecting on what they can complain about. You've heard it before, "You think your job stinks, just try mine." They complain because everything is not perfect or just the way they want it. Whiners make poor team players, so companies will rarely find them valuable for very long. It is often suggested to organization leaders that if they treat whiners and winners the same, sooner or later they will have more whiners than winners. If you find yourself whining, one remedy would be to just stop and press the delete button. Get your mind on to something positive. Count your blessings.

How many days do you get up in the morning and just don't want to go to work or take care of your children? Your mind is cluttered with all your worries, complaints, and insecurities. Your stress is high, you feel your boss doesn't appreciate you, and you're paid less than you deserve.

Many people seem to be born whiners and complainers. We suggest that you not spend too much time with them. The boss knows who they are. When he or she sees you with them what will happen? The boss will think you are a whiner too. In fact, you may well become one. People do assume the traits of those they associate with. Don't walk away from whiners—run away from them.

Another remedy to the tendency to whine is to focus on all that you have to be thankful for. Do you have a family? Do you have a job? Do you have a husband or wife who loves you? Remind yourself, that while your job is not perfect, you have a job. Be thankful. Remind yourself, that while your children may fight and fuss, there are many people who pray passionately every night to be able to have children just like yours. Be thankful. Remind yourself, that although you are not as handsome, beautiful, or rich as you may like to be, many others would trade places with you in a heartbeat. Remember to be thankful for your blessings. As Paul said (Philippians 2:14), "Do everything without complaining or arguing..." So, stop for a moment and express three things to yourself that you are thankful for. Do it now. The whining will fade away.

Think about the consequences of constant complaining. Watch and notice the people at your work. Is it the whiners who become leaders? Does whining gain your coworkers respect and give you a competitive edge? Just as there are examples of whiners all around you, you can also find heroic examples of people who stand up to the problems life presents them. An example of courage that everyone knows is that of Christopher Reeves. Known best as "Superman" he was a handsome, rising star in Hollywood. Yet few people knew how super he really was until a tragic horseriding accident left him paralyzed from the neck down. Such a loss would devastate almost anyone. But Christopher Reeves has repeatedly shown hope and encouragement since that accident. He has been an inspiration to millions. Likewise, when actor Michael J. Fox and Mohammed Ali developed Parkinson's disease, they didn't go into a closet. Instead, they both continue to show strength and pride while promoting research for a Parkinson's cure. But you don't have to be a TV or movie star to be such a hero. There are countless examples every day of normal people who choose to be winners instead of whiners. Try to take strength from these examples of courage, and be an example to others. Do you know a winner who had every right to be a whiner? What do you think of that person?

If you are to become more successful you must try to minimize your whining and complaining. They create a negative atmosphere. Dr. Wayne Dyer talks about two types of people. There are ducks who go around all day, quacking and complaining about their problems and never taking the time to solve them. And then there are eagles. Eagles fly and rise above their problems. So ask yourself everyday, am I a duck or an eagle? Be a person who identifies their problems, takes them on as a challenge, and takes action to solve them. If things need changing, then be a "mover and a shaker," rather than a complainer. Be the one who helps correct deficiencies and problems, rather than just complaining about them.

Realize that whining is more a bad habit than a true character flaw. Some people do great at work or school but whine and complain every night when they get home. Remember to show your best side to your loved ones as well as to your coworkers. If you have a bad habit of complaining, try to catch yourself the next time you whine and instead say something positive or helpful. Reflect in thankfulness on some of your blessings. Learning that whining is not winning is an important step towards improving your job performance and marriage, increasing self-esteem, and becoming a leader. Remember, there is a leader inside you. We have found that some people do not realize that about themselves. YOU ARE A LEADER.

* * * *

TRY THESE IDEAS:

1. Write down the three things you whine about most often. Decide on a different approach in these three areas.

2. The next time you find yourself complaining to someone, stop and tell them, "You know, it's not so bad. I'll be fine. Thanks for listening to me whine but I better move beyond the problem."

* * * *

Suggested Affirmation: Say out loud 10 times, "I am winning more, because I am whining less."

* * * *

Write down the most important thing(s) to remember from this Pearl:

_____

_____

_____

PEARL #21

—— ❧ ——

Look at Your Attitude

"The greatest discovery in life is that men can alter their life by altering their minds."
—**William James**

"The situation you live in doesn't have to live in you."
—**Roberta Flack**

"No one can make you feel inferior without your consent."
—**Eleanor Roosevelt**

"Our life is what our thoughts make it."
—**Marcus Aurelius**

* * * *

THIS BOOK TALKS a lot about attitude. That is because attitude is so important! As they say, your attitude will greatly affect your altitude in life. Did you know that? It is often said that attitude is our outward

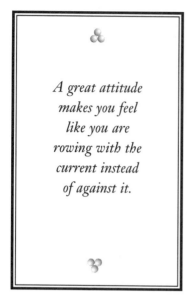

A great attitude makes you feel like you are rowing with the current instead of against it.

expression of how you feel inwardly. Do you need to take a look at some of your attitudes? Isn't it funny that the older you get, the more you realize how important a good attitude is. You realize this because it becomes so obvious in other people's lives that you eventually see it in your own. You eventually realize the huge advantage of a great attitude at school, work, and in your relationships at home.

A great attitude makes you feel like you are rowing with the current instead of against it. How can a person not have friends, find opportunities, or be happy if he or she has a great attitude? Keith Harrell, one of the country's rising motivational keynote speakers, says in his book, *Attitude Is Everything*, that a great way to improve your attitude is with a power greeting. He says every time he greets someone he says, "I'm super fantastic." In this way he makes people feel good and strengthens his own self-confidence. Power greetings help to engage others and shift energy to a positive state. This greeting may not be your style or may be over the top for you. That is okay. Develop your own power greeting and try it for twenty-one days (the time it takes to change a behavior). Dr. Judy Sundayo, a noted psychologist in San Diego, often uses a power greeting when asked how she is doing. She replies, "I feel close to excellent." Then she smiles, demonstrating a warmth that compels you to connect with her.

Your attitude is more important than where you come from. What difference does it make if you come from the USA, Cuba, or Russia if you don't take advantage of the great opportunities and freedoms in America by doing your best? There are people who escape war and poverty in distant lands, come to the USA, and become tremendously successful. More so than millions of people who have the lifelong advantage of having been born in America. How do these other people do it? For the most part, these are people with a great attitude towards hard work, opportunity, thoughtfulness, and persistence.

Leader after leader will say that a great attitude is more important than your education, certificates, and degrees. Does it really matter if you have a M.S. in Education if you do not have a loving heart for children? Does it matter if you have a law degree, but care little about justice? Formal education creates wonderful opportunities, but true excellence comes only if it is coupled with a great attitude. Doctors get very similar education, but differences in their attitudes often are what separate the great healers from the others.

Attitude is more important than all the money you have. Watch people closely. Rich people with a bad attitude have few friends and little happiness. Their poor attitude may even cause them to blow all their money, ruin their health with drugs or gluttony, and destroy relationships by reckless and self-centered lifestyles. A great attitude can bring you both wealth and happiness. It can make your marriage and relationships more special.

In some of Brian Tracy's and Earl's workshops or seminars they ask their audiences the question, "How many of you are self-employed?" Few people raise their hands. They then ask again, and again, and again until everyone gets the point. Everyone is self-employed! If you work at the post office you are self-employed because you are selling your service to the post office. You decide if you go to work there. If you are a teacher, you are self-employed. No one forces you to be a teacher. You do it because that is what you want to do and hopefully for the love of children. Remember, children need your caring more than they do your knowledge. You decide if the conditions of employment and your pay are acceptable.

It is YOU, Inc. So even the concept of "self-employment" is more of an attitude than a tax-related definition. And it feels good to realize you are self-employed, doesn't it? This self-employed attitude translates into a "I'm making a contribution" attitude. It fires up a "can do" attitude.

Anyone who has ever been a leader or manager of a group of people understands the huge value of great attitudes. It makes the leader's job easier, the team better, and the people on the team happier. Great attitudes by employees move teams forward and bad ones hold teams back like an anchor. People with great attitudes have high self-esteem, more creativity, more enthusiasm, and tend to see the positives in any situation. It will greatly enhance your performance. If you are a parent, you know the importance of attitude. What a joy it is to have a child with a great attitude, and what hardships can develop when a child has an "attitude problem."

What is your attitude at home? Do you bring joy and comfort to your spouse and children? Do they get the best you? It is your memories with your family that you will cherish most. If you are in school, do you have an attitude of learning or are you just doing what you have to do in order to pass? An attitude of learning is actually much more fun than being lazy. It is hard work being behind at school and trying to catch up at the end of the semester. Find a good attitude of learning even in the classes you are not naturally interested in. Anyone can rise to the occasion in the classes they enjoy. The people with the highest grades are not always the smartest. They are people who worked hard in all their classes,

> *A great attitude correlates better with success than almost any other attribute.*

whether they enjoyed them or not. Often if you try harder at a subject you will enjoy it more because you understand it more. *A great attitude correlates better with success than almost any other attribute.*

Talk to any coach and you'll hear how important a great attitude is to their team. A great attitude means being a team player. As the saying goes, there is no "I" in "Team." Having a good attitude means being enthusiastic, hard working, and willing to learn. It also means doing the right thing, even if many others are not. It means making work more fun. Employers will pay a lot of money for people they really want to keep. Those people are the ones who are talented, work hard, and possess a great attitude. John Maxwell, a leadership guru, offers several attitude remedy ideas for leaders in his leadership series. "Say the right things." "Listen to the right audiotapes." "Read the right books." "Associate with the right people." "Do the right thing." Wow! If you can just follow this simple plan, your family life and workplace will be so much better. Dr. Maxwell further relates that your attitude is affected by three F's: your friendship, failures, and (view of the) future. Take a moment and reflect on your feelings in each of these areas. What did you discover?

* * * *

TRY THESE IDEAS:

1. Find one way to improve your attitude at work and put it into action.

2. Find one way to improve your attitude at home. Start today! Why wait?

3. Ask someone close to you how they think you can improve in your attitude.

* * * *

Suggested Affirmation: Say out loud 10 times, "My attitude at home and at work is becoming better every day."

* * * *

Write down the most important thing(s) to remember from this Pearl:

PEARL #22

&

Embrace Positive Change

"You must be the change you wish to see in the world."
—Mahatma Gandhi

"Change your thoughts, you can change your world."
—Ralph Waldo Emerson

"If we want to change a situation we first have to change ourselves, and to change ourselves effectively we have to change our perspective."
—Steven Covey

* * * *

WHEN WAS THE LAST TIME you made a significant change in your life? Are you changing now? Are you making good positive changes for your life as you work through this book? In what ways are you trying to improve yourself? These are some of the questions you need to ask yourself.

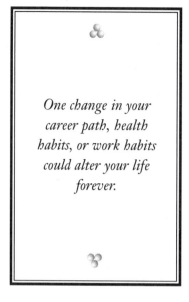

One change in your career path, health habits, or work habits could alter your life forever.

We are not talking about easy way out changes, or change for change's sake. We are not talking about idle restlessness, reckless changes, mid-life crises. We are talking about change that leads to growth and personal development. Change for change's sake, if not dangerous, is meaningless. However, change for mental, physical, and spiritual growth is extremely valuable. *One change in your career path, health habits, or work habits could alter your life forever.* For example, reducing the amount of alcohol you drink, cutting back on all the ice cream you eat, or deciding to jog daily could add years and better health to your life. Successful people develop good, *everyday* habits such as exercise, reading, and quiet reflection time. Re-inventing your career path may lead to more opportunities, greater joy, and more wealth than you ever imagined. As Peter Drucker has said, "If you are through changing, you are through."

You may be going through some important changes right now. Perhaps some changes in life are good and others are not. Ask yourself if the changes you are going through right now will make you more content five years from now, or will they leave a path of hurt? Will they make your spouse, children, parents, and friends proud of you? Is your change consistent with your goals, family values, and your faith? Are they directions or changes that you would recommend to your children? These are questions that you can use to determine whether you are on the right path as you make changes. Remember, changes can be good or bad, heartening or corrupting.

It is important to remember that some changes are painful at first, but pay off later. For example, leaving a full-time job to go back to school may increase your financial difficulties for several years, but later it may bring huge benefits that could last a lifetime. Being able to delay gratification is a characteristic of a mature person. It is vital to success. You don't have to (or want to) wait for all rewards, but some take time to develop. Usually these are the best ones. Moving to a new home or even a job promotion can be extremely stressful at first, only to yield great rewards down the road. Visualizing where your changes will lead one, five, and ten years down the road is therefore vital. Reflect and think it through. Let your inner goodness and heart be your guide.

Change comes in three basic types. One is a change in **knowledge**. You may be gaining some knowledge from reading this book, talking with your boss, or from any number of sources. Formal education is certainly a rapid way to acquire knowledge (and it comes with a diploma as proof!). If your formal education is incomplete, consider ways to complete it. For some people this may mean taking night classes to finish a college degree. For others it means going on to an MBA or a law degree. Rarely will you meet someone who says, "Boy, I wish I had less education." Many very bright people are stuck in their jobs because they haven't completed the formal education level they need to go to the next level within their organization. If you are one of these people, don't waste your time about how unfair it is. Instead, get the education you need and compete effectively.

> *It is important to remember that some changes are painful at first, but pay off later.*

The second is changes in **attitude**. If you are a supervisor you already know the high value of this one. Having employees with a good attitude is a true blessing to a manager. There is even a ripple effect: A positive attitude in you affects other people's attitudes and ignites a forward momentum for the entire group. Changes in attitude will affect every aspect of your life. Although we have already discussed the great importance of attitude in a previous Pearl, it cannot be emphasized enough. Your attitude will greatly affect your relationships, success, and happiness.

Because it is so vital, attitude is a major component in every Pearl of this book.

Finally there is the change in **behavior**. That's probably the toughest one, isn't it? It's hard changing your patterns of behavior. But not enough can be said for having the discipline to develop and carry out good habits every day. This often means changing the way you've been thinking as well. An alcoholic must truly *decide* to stop drinking in order to change his or her behavior. Old habits are hard to break and take real effort, discipline, and determination. Sometimes it requires one to make changes in the friends he hangs out with. In the substance abuse field this is referred to as "changing playgrounds and playmates." Some people will never "grow up" if they stay with the same immature buddies. As Paul states, "When I was a child, I talked like a child, I thought like a child, I reasoned like a child. When I became a man, I put childish ways behind me" (1 Corinthians 13:11). What behaviors do you need to change? Do you need to change your eating habits, smoking habits, or exercise program? Think it through.

Changes can be hard. An important trick to change is the concept "Fake it, 'til you make it." This goes back to our concept of reprogramming your mind. If you act confident, you will become more confident. If you act happy, you will become happier. So be now (even if it takes effort) what you want to be later! Going to work is an excellent example of this concept. How many times did you not want to be at work, but acted as if you did anyway? Eventually your attitude changed because you faked it! It works. And why let only the people at work enjoy the best you? Let your family also enjoy the best of you. Put a smile on your face at home as well.

Try changing a small aspect of your physical appearance right now (such as your hairstyle). Does it feel strange? The first thing to remember about change is that changes in your life may feel awkward at first. That's all right. That's normal. Now try imagining three changes in your personal dress or appearance. The changes can be small or big. Did you start by taking something off? Sometimes change is removing things in your life. Some things in your life are like weights that hold you back. Examples might include smoking, drugs, or even old resentments. You could also have added something (like a hat) when you imagined changing your appearance. Getting married, having children, or completing your education are some major add-on changes. Sometimes when people think of change, they think only of loss. That's why a lot of people don't want to change.

If you do lose something important when you make a change, go ahead and mourn the loss. Some degree of grieving is normal and healthy. But after mourning the loss, push yourself to move on. Changing jobs for example, brings new excitement, but it also requires leaving people and places you know. There is nothing wrong with feeling sad about those losses, but don't let it consume you or get in the way of enjoying your new opportunities. It is also important to remind yourself that people who are truly important to you have more ways than ever to keep in touch. Cell phones, e-mail, and two-way radios (who knows what's next!) make the world a lot smaller.

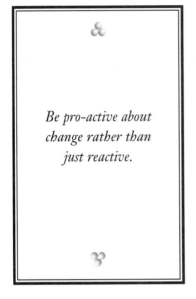

Be pro-active about change rather than just reactive.

Change often comes whether you like it or not. Watch children grow up. They change and have to leave many things behind along the way in order to develop into a mature man or woman. Some of the things you left behind were fun (such as playing with dolls or other toys) but were meant for a child. Change is the way of things. But just don't sit back and always wait for change to come to you. If it comes to you, you won't know what to expect. It may feel like a tidal wave hitting you. *Be pro-active about change rather than just reactive.* Take control of the changes in your life and the positive changes you make will feel like a refreshing swim. Growing old is something everyone experiences (if he or she is lucky enough). However, try to take control over your aging experience by making good choices now. An interesting t-shirt bore the following phrase: "Aging: Only the best people are doing it." How true! Sort of makes you think about aging differently, doesn't it? A great attitude helps keep you young.

If we had asked you to imagine making ten changes in your personal appearance, how would you feel? "Oh my gosh," you would think! That would be too many changes! When you are making changes in your life, don't make too many at once. Only make one or two changes at a time. The problem with a lot of people is that they try to make too many changes at once and it can be overwhelming to them. Change may also require patience. You may want change to come faster but it won't. Many significant changes come only after long, patient effort. Physicians must attend medical school for four years (after four years of college) and residency training afterwards for three to seven years. It isn't easy, but their effort is usually well rewarded. Likewise, a rigorous exercise program will not reduce your weight or build up your biceps overnight. But give it time and exercise is one of the most reliable tools for positive physical change and mental health. Thus, change may require slow determined effort, rather than reckless risk taking or unrealistic expectations.

Sometimes when people make changes there is a tendency to revert back to old behaviors. When you find yourself reverting back to old behaviors that you know you need to avoid ask yourself, "Isn't that interesting? I am going back to my old behaviors. Why in the world would I do that?" Perhaps you are reverting back into an old relationship with a toxic, corrupting person. Perhaps you are excessively using alcohol or drugs again. So be careful of changes that push you in a detrimental direction. Be sure your changes lead to growth, not regression. Be sure they are good, not harmful. Keep your spiritual life in all of your life.

We often talk to people who want to change their life, but won't expend the necessary effort. If you want to improve, you have got to invest in your changes. It may mean investing in your education or in a business. It may mean spending more time at the gym or with your spouse or your children. Many people want others to change so that they don't have to. These people are usually disappointed, because the world will usually not change for you. This means you must take the initiative. Sometimes you just need to make a few minor changes in your life. It might mean spending a little more time reading books, going to church, taking courses, going to seminars, or spending time with a mentor. It might mean going on evening walks with your husband or wife to enhance your communication and relationship. Perhaps you need to spend an extra hour each night playing with your toddler. Have the courage, energy, and enthusiasm to change in positive directions.

* * * *

TRY THESE IDEAS:

1. Write down the last major positive change you made that helped you grow. What did you learn?

2. Write down the last major change you made that hurt you. What did you learn from it, and how can you prevent a similar mistake?

3. Write down one change you need to make in the future in the areas of knowledge, attitude, behavior, and relationships.

* * * *

Suggested Affirmation: Say out loud 10 times, "I am changing for the better each day and it feels good."

* * * *

Write down the most important thing(s) to remember from this Pearl:

_____

_____

_____

PEARL # 2 3

Be an
Asking Person

*"Ask and it shall be given to you; seek and
ye shall find, knock and the door shall be
opened to you ... For everyone who asks receives."*
—Jesus Christ, Matthew 7:7-8, Bible

"You have to ASK if you want to GET."
—Jack Canfield

* * * *

I N ORDER TO GROW and improve you have to continue
to learn. In order to learn, you have to find answers. *In order
to find answers, you have to ASK QUESTIONS!* How can you
find answers without asking questions? How many people ask
for help? In doing seminars on change, Earl asks his audiences
about the most difficult aspect of change. The universal response is
"asking for help." Some men seem to be especially prone to "going
it alone." That may sound heroic, but it's probably why so many
men get stuck at a place far below their potential. Ask their wives,
they know! Their pride gets in the way. Are you stuck below your

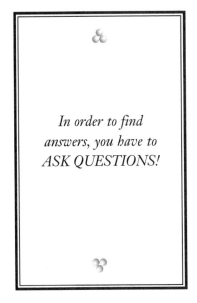

In order to find answers, you have to ASK QUESTIONS!

potential? Are you asking enough important questions in order to get the important answers you need?

Perhaps you are not sure what questions you should be asking or what sort of help you need. Ask the questions at work that will give you new insights. Ask people who have been successful at your work, "How did you do it?" Ask questions that will help you develop new skills and expertise. You can choose to do the same job over and over for years, or you can ask questions to find out ways to move up in your company.

You may have to ask for a promotion to get one. Did you know it often works that way? Why should your boss give you a promotion if you seem happy to do the same job for less? Perhaps your boss just hasn't thought about it. You may know that you've been there for five years without a raise, but he or she may not have thought about it. For example, Dr. Hubbard was pleasantly surprised on those times he asked for raises and got them, but what was most instructive was the realization that had he not *asked* for them, they would not have been offered. So even though you may be worth more money, chances are no one will volunteer to give it to you. You won't get everything you ask for, but some of what you ask for may make a big difference.

Do you know you have to "no" your way to the top? *You've got to be able to accept a lot of "no's" to get some important "yes's."* In fact, after a few "no's" your supervisor may feel it is time for a "yes." If you aren't willing to hear "no," then you are not ready to ask. If you can handle "yes" or "no" then asking will be no problem. You've got to take a lot of "no's" if you want to be successful. That is because some answers will be "yes." "Yes, you can be on that project." "No, you can't work on that one now." "Yes, you can have a raise." "No, you can't get a new corner office." "Yes, you can have time off for your sick child." "No, you can't take two weeks off straight." One "yes" may land you a job that changes your entire career or give you important time with your family. It may get you a promotion or a raise that your entire family will benefit from.

Begin by asking someone to be a mentor to you. You will need a special person to mentor you. Most people would love to teach you what they know. Mentors should be people who are most likely to give you honest and useful answers to your questions. They should be knowledgeable, positive, and caring people. In most cases it is best to choose a mentor who is the same gender as you. Once you have a mentor, he or she will be a source of answers to many of your questions. This is so important, that we devote an entire "Pearl" to mentors and networks.

Ask your husband or wife what they want and need from you. Believe it or not, you may not know! Even after 10, 20, or 30 years of marriage many spouses don't know what their husband or wife really wants or needs from them. Perhaps you've been trying to solve a problem your spouse has complained about when all he or she really needs is for you to truly listen and understand. Perhaps you are a housewife that shows your love to your husband by devotion to your children. However, if you ask him you may find that your husband really wants more time alone with you. Maybe you are a husband who

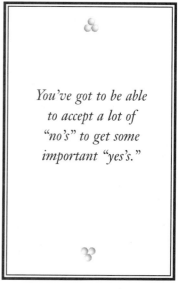

You've got to be able to accept a lot of "no's" to get some important "yes's."

can't wait to build your wife a new house, but what she really wants is a smaller gift of affection now.

Ask how you can reduce your spouse's stress and reduce some of their load. Perhaps you don't want to ask your spouse what they need because you don't want to know. If that is the case, you may need to examine whether you are doing your full part in your marriage? Maybe you need to ask your spouse what pleases them in the bedroom. Even after many years, sex and romance are important to a marriage. Ask your husband or wife what they enjoy. Perhaps they need more comforting or perhaps some new ways of excitement. You'd be surprised how many husbands and wives don't know because they don't ask. Ask how your spouse is doing every day. Really listen. When you listen well, your spouse will notice. It builds trust and understanding and raises their self-esteem. After listening, you can problem-solve together.

At one seminar Earl was given a list of "God's Emergency Phone Numbers." It seemed like a useful idea, so we have come up with a list of our own, as shown below:

When in sad or depressed — call Isaiah 25:8, Isaiah 41:10, Psalms 50:15, 1 John 4:4, 2 Corinthians 7:6

When fearful — call Isaiah 41:10, Mark 5:36, Phillipians 4:6-7, 1 John 3:18, 1 Peter 5:7

When you need confidence against sin — call Romans 8:9, 1 Corinthians 10:13

When you have worry — call Phillipians 4:6-7

When you want more out of life — call John 10:10

When God seems distant — call 1 Corinthians 3:16, 1 Corinthians 5:4

When you feel lonely — *call 2 Corinthians 12:9, Matthew 28:20, I John 4:12-15*

When you feel overburdened — *call Matthew 28:30*

When you feel weak — *call 2 Corinthians 12:9*

When you need confidence — *call Ephesians 3:20, Luke 1:37, Matthew 19:26, James 1:6, James 4:16*

When you need comfort — *call John 14:1*

When you need help — *call Matthew 7:7-8*

When you are in trouble — *call Psalms 50:15, James 5:13*

When you need strength — *call Psalms 18:2, Phillipians 4:13, John 9:31*

When you need faith — *call Mark 11:22-24, James 1:6, Matthew 21:21*

The emergency numbers above may be dialed direct. No operator assistance is necessary. And as always, the call is toll-free. Read the Bible and develop your personal list of emergency numbers. Ask God what he wants and expects from you. Ask how you can be of better use to God. All lines are open to heaven 24 hours a day! Feed your faith, starve your doubt.

So be an asking person at home, in prayer, and at work. Don't pester people, but keep asking until you get the "yes" that can change your life. That one special "yes" may get you a promotion, improve your marriage, or help you obtain a new job.

* * * *

TRY THESE IDEAS:

1. Ask your husband, wife, or other loved one what they need from you but are not getting. Care enough to really listen.

2. Ask questions at work that will give you more knowledge and value to the company.

3. Ask a person who has gotten to where you want to go to be your mentor.

4. Ask God what change He desires of you.

* * * *

Suggested Affirmation: Say out loud 10 times, "I'm becoming a better asking person. Reaching out for God's help and other people's help is a strength, not a weakness."

* * * *

Write down the most important thing(s) to remember from this Pearl:

_____

_____

_____

PEARL # 24

Practice the Law of Giving

"Each man should give what he has decided
in his heart to give, not reluctantly or
under compulsion, for God loves a cheerful giver."
—Paul, 2 Corinthians 9:7, Bible

"The greatest gifts my parents gave to me...were
their unconditional love and a set of values.
Values that they lived and didn't just lecture about."
—Colin Powell

"The purpose of human life is to serve and
to show compassion and the will to help others."
—Albert Schweitzer

"There is no happiness in having or in getting,
but only in giving."
—Henry Drummond

* * * *

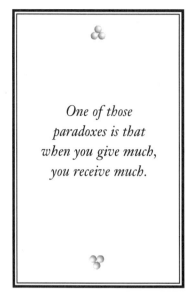

> *One of those paradoxes is that when you give much, you receive much.*

THE WORLD HAS many paradoxes. *One of those paradoxes is that when you give much, you receive much.* Truly happy people understand this law. They love to give. On the other hand, very serious consequences can occur if you don't give effectively in your life. This "Law of Giving" is an important concept because it will help bring you joy and success. Joyful receiving requires joyful giving. As Denny Miller said, "Happiness is a by-product of helping others."

People who are successful recognize that in order to keep their success, they have to give some of it away! It is important to give and share success with others. To get more in the future you must give more. This not only serves as an investment in others, but nourishes your heart and soul. Think back at the many nice gifts you have received and given. We bet you can remember the nice gifts you gave someone much more readily than you can remember the nice gifts you received. Isn't that true? Why is that? It is because you actually felt greater joy in giving than you did in receiving. *Although receiving is a natural consequence of giving, giving does not mean looking for something in return.* Not only does that diminish the gift and the spiritual aspect of

> *Although receiving is a natural consequence of giving, giving does not mean looking for something in return.*

giving, but it leads to disappointments when you do not receive things in return. Give unconditionally. As Jesus says, "But when you give to the needy, do not let your left hand know what your right hand is doing, so that your giving may be in secret. Then your Father, who sees what is done in secret, will reward you" (Matthew 6:3-4). Giving is a reward in and of itself. But don't be surprised if the more you give the more you receive. It is a law of nature, like gravity. It cannot be stopped. Give unconditionally and your spirit will grow and you will never be disappointed . Giving is not bargain making. It is being a blessing to someone else, and thus a blessing to your own spirit.

You may be thinking, "But what do I have to give? I am too poor, or I am too old, or I am too young." Everyone has something to give. If you are young, you have energy, strength, and fresh new ideas. If you are older, you have vast experience to share. You may have more to teach other people than you ever imagined. A very precious gift that you can give is your attention. Most people want to feel important enough to be noticed and listened to. You can help people just by listening to them! And guess what? You'd be sur-prised how much it can mean to people to give them some attention and empathy. Children love to tell their stories to someone, and so do adults. A major complaint children have about parents is that they don't listen more to them. *Everyone has something to give because everyone can listen and give thoughtful attention to other people.* So being old, young, rich, or poor is not an excuse to neglect giving someone your ear.

> &
>
> *Everyone has something to give because everyone can listen and give thoughtful attention to other people.*
>
> ℘

Some people have more money and possessions than others and so they may be able to give more material things as well. That is great. You may have money to offer to a needy person, church, or a good cause. The Bible stresses tithing as a form of financial giving; the Old Testament states that God wants you go give 10% of your income to the church. Jesus also endorses this but adds that the attitude of giving is even more important than the amount. You must have the heart for giving when you tithe or when you give.

Maybe it is your knowledge of how you obtained wealth that someone needs to learn. Be known as the person who cares, teaches, and tries to help others. As they say, give someone a fish and you feed them for one day. Teach them to fish, and you feed them for a lifetime. You may be able to help someone's career or relieve a coworker's stress. There are so many big and little ways to give. Be creative.

Give bountifully in small but meaningful ways. Give your smile away often. Smiles help to brighten a room, a conversation, and relationships. Give away your thanks. Tell people "thank you" without hesitation. People need to know they are appreciated. Give away small gifts and hugs and kisses to loved ones. Hold your husband's or wife's hand and snuggle them close when you sit down together after a long day. Give your love to them whether they "deserve" it that day or not. This form of giving is free and yet worth more than gold. It tells people that you care about them.

Dr. Hubbard often tells his patients to think of their consciousness (their thoughts) as a bright light. If you are self-centered and always have that light shining on yourself what will happen? You will get burned! That is one of the ways people develop anxiety problems, self-consciousness, and perhaps even depression. Such people worry and obsess far too much about themselves. Dr. Hubbard tells them that by shining the light of their attention (or consciousness) out towards others, they can help warm the world! Helping others always feels good and is a vital component of moving towards excellence. And in the end, helping others is what it's all about, isn't it?

Be a seed planter who plants seeds of ideas and encouragement in other people's lives and watch what happens to your good works. The difference you make in this world has much to do with how much you give. So find creative ways to give more. The more you give the more will come back to you. It will come without asking. It will make you feel great! Giving is an important part of the journey to success, joy, and excellence.

*   *   *   *

TRY THESE IDEAS:

1. Give something unexpected to a friend or loved one today.

2. Give a smile to someone at work who looks like they could use one.

3. Evaluate where your financial charity is going. Is it getting to the people who need it most?

*   *   *   *

Suggested Affirmation: Say 10 times out loud, "I give to others because it is right. But by doing so I receive more also."

*   *   *   *

Write down the most important thing(s) to remember from this Pearl:

_____

_____

_____

PEARL # 25

⊹

Find Mentors and Build Networks

"Imitation is the sincerest form of flattery."
—Charles Caleb Colton

"Relationships have more to do with your success than anything else."
—Terrie Williams

"The jockey that wins the race is usually the one with the best horse."
—Al Ries and Jack Trout

* * * *

IT HAS BEEN SAID that part of the overall business strategy of many companies today is mentoring (both informally and formally). Top management recognizes in these turbulent times of change and transition that they desperately need to develop and empower leaders at all levels within their organiza-

Mentors are those special people such as parents, spouses, teachers, friends, bosses, coworkers, coaches, and senior people who act as role models, nurture, advise, and/or take you under their wing.

tion if they are going to survive, thrive, and have a competitive advantage. *Mentors are those special people such as parents, spouses, teachers, friends, bosses, coworkers, coaches, and senior people who act as role models, nurture, advise, and/or take you under their wing.* They help you find solutions to obstacles in both your work and life. They may even help you crystallize the important questions to ask.

As you grew up, your most important mentors were your parent(s) (or other caretakers). Your parents not only sacrificed and provided for you, but they taught you about right from wrong and about unconditional love. Many parents do much more and play a direct role such as schoolteacher, coach and so on. Unfortunately there are others who do not mentor enough or teach by bad example. Parents are vital mentors. They can get their children off in the right direction and build their fragile self-esteems, or they can make life a far greater struggle for their offspring. If you are a parent, realize that it is one of the most important jobs you will ever have. Be a great mentor and role model to your children while they are young and later when they are adults. Remember that do what you do not what you say. Also remember showing love to them will cover many of your own shortfalls.

While you were in school you had many teachers and coaches, some of whom may have acted as a mentor to you. But you also need mentors after your formal education is over to help guide you to your next career level. If you go back and look at the "Acknowledgments" in this book you will see that we have had numerous mentors in many formal and informal settings. We can not thank those mentors, and many others, enough. It is vital that you find special people to teach you.

Do you have a mentor or mentors? Do you have people who teach you regularly, help you make better career choices, and help make your path smoother and faster by sharing their experiences and hearing your ideas? Do you have mentors for your spiritual life to help keep your direction on good paths? One of Dr. Hubbard's most cherished mentors (outside of his wife, parents and children) is Pastor Guy Holloway, who lives in Richmond, Virginia. They met about twenty years ago when Dr. Hubbard was walking his newborn daughter, Tara, and Pastor Holloway (a junior pastor then) was walking his newborn daughter late one night. They became friends during their nighttime walks and debated religion, as well as many other topics. After about a year of debate, through God's grace, Dr. Hubbard changed his attitude from that of a rigorous debater to that of an eager student. The value of such a spiritual mentor is beyond measure. They can do you more good than you could ever imagine. Having spiritual mentors (such as a minister or church elder) is a good idea if you want to avoid a lot of mistakes, detours, and roadblocks.

We suggest that before you seek a mentor, consider being a mentor to someone first. People certainly should both have mentors and be mentors to others. Author Wayne Dyer suggests having an attitude toward others that says, "How can I service you or how can I help you?" This is part of the "Law Of Giving" we talked about in a previous Pearl. Always ask yourself, "Am I bringing out the best in others?" Mary Kay, the founder of Mary Kay Products, says we should treat everyone we meet as though they have a sign on them that says, "Please, make me feel important." If you are constantly doing that, you will find yourself on the fast track towards finding and being a mentor. The giving path is far more rewarding than the "What can I get" path. Wendy Reed Crisp, National Director for

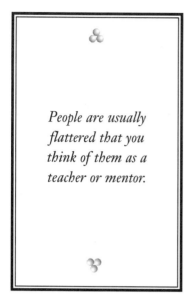

People are usually flattered that you think of them as a teacher or mentor.

NAFE (National Association of Female Executives), says, "The key to mentoring is our immortality. It is not in our success, it is the success of our protégées." She adds, "We feel if you want a safety net support system, you first must become a safety net for others." Mentoring others allows you to be a leader in a world whose organizations are constantly changing.

One of the first people you might consider for a mentor is your boss or someone else high in your organization. Some of you may say, "My boss is not a mentor—he or she is my tormentor." Why consider your boss? Because you may want to know what he or she knows, so that one day you can move up to a position like theirs. Mentors act as accelerators that help get you where you want to go faster. They help put you on the fast track to success. Your job should not be focused only on what you are doing there, but also on what you are learning there. If your boss is a tormentor, or toxic in some way to you, then do do not hesitate to look elsewhere. But a mentor at your workplace can be extremely valuable.

Look around you. Who can teach you the things you need to learn? A potential mentor may be twenty years your junior, but he or she may be able to teach you how to use computers or other technologies. A possible mentor may be twenty years older than you with a lot of experience. Don't be afraid to directly ask people to be your mentor, or to spend a little time with you discussing your ideas and their experience. *People are usually flattered that you think of them as a teacher or mentor.* A great way to get mentoring advice might be to go to someone you respect and ask, "I was wondering about this and and that. What do you think?"

It is generally best to find a same-sex mentor. (In case you read that fast, we did not say to get a sexy mentor. We said a mentor of the same sex as you.) Finding a mentor is not about being near a person you are attracted to, could become attracted to, or is attracted to you (such situations can really back-fire), but about finding a person who helps your professional or personal growth. In most cases, men should learn how to be successful from men. And likewise, so as to prevent misunderstandings, women would be best advised to find appropriate female mentors. Finding an excellent mentor for you can make a huge difference in the effectiveness of the plans you develop for your future.

It has been said that 75% of all jobs come from networking and 10% of all friendships come through networking. Networks of supportive people are vital. Do not underestimate the power of associations in your life. When you become supportive to others, others come out of the woodwork to support you. You know the old saying, "It is not what you know, but who you know." That may be a cynical or broad statement, but it does contain some truth. Put another way, it really isn't whom you know, but WHO KNOWS YOU! Someone needs to know you before they can have confidence in you. They really want to know about your attitude and how much you care about working. Would you want to hire someone you'd briefly met during two interviews, or someone who made a good impression over several meetings? In *Swim With the Sharks*, Harvey McKay suggests keeping a Rolodex file on people you meet because you never know when you might need someone. People remember you if you remember them. Similarly, Tom Peters advises being a "Rolodex maniac" to help you become successful.

To write this book, we needed a network of reviewers. The most amazing thing about looking at the advice of reviewers (from both this book and others) is how different it can be. No one is right or wrong, but they all see things in different ways and have unique ideas. That is why several reviewers are needed for a book. They all bring different insights, talents, and backgrounds to the table. We are so thankful for the diversity of our reviewers. As a writer, it is humbling to know that you can look at a page twenty-plus times and still miss something obvious to a reviewer. But that is why you need a network: to focus on areas that may fall in your "blind spot" and get fresh, new ideas and valuable feedback. After you receive someone's business card, a simple follow-up call—just to say hello and ask how they're doing—can make a great difference in the start a successful business relationship. Also, consider creating your own website. More and more these days, computer technology is used to initiate business relationships.

Spousal mentoring (i.e. mentoring from our spouses) is an area often overlooked because spouses are so close to each other's lives. However, we believe one of the most important mentors you can ever have is your wife or husband. Both Dr. Hubbard and Earl have been immensely blessed by the things they have learned from their wives. As Dr. Hubbard readily tells people, he had been described (at best) as a "diamond in the rough" when his wife Suzanne met him in college. Having grown up the fifth of ten children, social skills at his house were primarily not doing bodily harm to other siblings or overt destruction of the house. He considered velvet paintings to be true works of art and he was totally clueless how to dress well. Fortunately for Dr. Hubbard, Suzanne helped to set new direction and standards in these and other areas. Eventually, Sue taught him how to match clothing and about more refined taste in many areas from art to furniture. By her example, advice, confidence, and encouragement, Dr. Hubbard has moved through many exciting phases of his career. Suzanne's zest for life and natural understanding of parenting has helped her husband learn how to be a better father and to enjoy many aspects of life that may not have been obvious without her. (Thanks Sue!).

Likewise, Earl too is a student of his wife. Felicia taught him how to grow professionally and network "like crazy." She taught him the value of keeping a Rolodex file for both business and personal relationships "just to stay in touch." She further taught Earl how to dress for success that he values to this day. Even on air flights Earl likes to dress well (as you never know whom you may meet). As Felicia has taught him, "First impressions continue to always be the last impression." Felicia also always encourages Earl to read and learn methods to interact well with others. Encouragement to others and personal warmth are the hallmarks Earl strives for. So don't forget that your spouse is not only your life mate, but also your mentor. (Thanks Felicia!).

Associations have a great influence on your life. Your associations impact your attitude as well. There is no doubt about it. People can open doors for you. They can introduce you to other people. There is power in associations with other people. Look at the animal kingdom. Animals of smaller size can defeat a larger animal if they hunt in packs. When you join a group, its members strengthen you and you strengthen them. So pay attention to those ahead of you, but don't neglect your "lesser" associations. You might think, "Oh, that little person doesn't matter." But remember how easily people can affect your reputation: word about your kindness (or the lack thereof) and trustworthiness travels fast. As Wendy Crisp, Director of NAFE says, "There are no unimportant people." People know whom to turn to for help in a corporation. Things are often said when you are well out of earshot. Make the things said of you good things. The way you treat "junior" associations defines your true character, more so than how you treat higher-ups. Try to make everyone you see regularly feel like they are important to you, whether they be your boss or the person cleaning your office.

Remember our discussion about toxic people? If you see that the people you associate with are toxic to you, separate yourself from them as quickly as possible! Associates can have positive or negative effects on you. What happens if you associate with people who spend all their money in bars? Sooner or later, you'll be buying rounds at "Happy Hour." Hang around drug users long enough and you'll find yourself using, too. (In the substance abuse field this is called the "cocaine dance".) And if you spend time with people who have affairs, eventually marital infidelity won't seem that wrong. But if you associate with people who are faithful, ambitious, hard working, and strong in spirit, you will soon exhibit the same traits.

Have you ever heard of the PHD syndrome? The PHD stands for "Pull Him (or Her) Down." Toxic people will pull you down. They will pour cold water on your dreams and ideas if you let them. Toxic people will tell you how things can't be done. They will take you to places you shouldn't go. They will ask you to do things that you shouldn't do. Don't be tempted; be strong. As Paul says in 1 Corinthians 10:13, "No temptation has seized you except what is common to man. And God is faithful: he will not let you be tempted beyond what you can bear. But when you are tempted, he will also provide a way out so that you can stand up under it." Do you remember the movie, "Ghostbusters"? There are "dream busters" out there. Toxic people will bust your dreams if you let them. Develop a healthy network of associates and stay clear of toxic people.

Finally, we want to remind you that the best counselors you will ever have are the Father, Son and Holy Spirit. Prayer, faith and biblical reading are wonderful sources of this counseling. In Isaiah 9:6 of the Old Testament it is said, "For to us a child is born, to us a son is given... and he will be called Wonderful Counselor, Mighty God, Everlasting Father, Prince of Peace." Later, Jesus says, "And I will ask the Father, and He will give you another Counselor to be with you forever — the Spirit of Truth." (John 14:16). He also adds, "But the counselor, or, the Holy Spirit, whom the Father will send in my name, will teach you all things and will remind you of everything I have said to you." (John 14:26). So have faith and grace; let God teach you and be your guide in all things.

* * * *

TRY THESE IDEAS:

1. Offer yourself to be a mentor for someone. Always respond with enthusiasm if someone asks you for help.

2. Ask someone to be a mentor for you at work.

3. Ask yourself who are you not spending time with that you should. Call that person(s) and make some time together. Stay in touch with them, asking for nothing.

4. Take some reflection time and make a list of the people you associate with. Then ask yourself, should I move toward them or away from them?

* * * *

Suggested Affirmations: Say out loud 10 times, "I enjoy being a mentor and I enjoying having a mentor."

* * * *

Write down the most important thing(s) to remember from this Pearl:

_____

_____

_____

_____

PEARL #26

Develop Hobbies and Exercise

"Finding your hobby can lead you to your passion in life."
—Carol Hyatt

"Where your interests are, there is your energy also."
—Dale Carnegie

* * * *

STRESS (MORE PROPERLY CALLED "DISTRESS") can drain your energy, dull your mind, destroy your relationships, and deflate your spirit. It doesn't matter if you are a housewife, policeman, soldier, doctor, teacher, factory worker, or corporate executive—stress will find you and you will have to develop effective ways to deal with it. A group of corporate executives were reportedly asked, "How do you deal with all the stress on your job?" Guess what most of them said? "Hobbies." The survey also asked what do their hobbies have to do with their jobs? The most common answer was, nothing. That's the point. You have to do some things outside of your job that allows you to unwind.

Yes, striving for excellence means having some fun!

Do you have a hobby that allows you to get away from your work (or housework) and other stressors? Do you have a hobby that lets you take a break from your chores and responsibilities? *Yes, striving for excellence means having some fun!* Hobbies serve primarily to relax your mind by focusing it on something other than your work and worries. In this way, hobbies resemble meditation. They should be fun, keep you focused, and make you feel relaxed. For some people this means knitting, gardening, golf, photography, model building, computer games, boating, carpentry, basketball, hunting, fishing, or a thousand other activities. The key is to have a hobby, one that puts a smile on your face.

Start a hobby now so that your love and talent for it have time to grow. People with hobbies always have something to look forward to. They never have to worry about being bored. For some people, retirement can be a bigger stress than work. Many people become couch potatoes, lose self-esteem, and become depressed after they retire. Hobbies help keep people from losing interest in life. After you retire, it may be one of the main things that gets you up in the morning and makes you sleep better at night. We are not saying that retire-

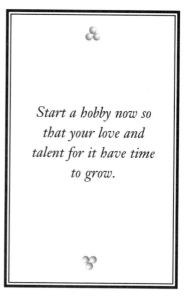

Start a hobby now so that your love and talent for it have time to grow.

ment is something to fear. On the contrary, it can give you the freedom to do the things you really want to do and the time to do them. Our point is only that you should start developing hobbies before you retire so that you can better enjoy them afterwards.

Consider at least one hobby that you can do on your own. Playing on the computer, working on cars, painting, writing, cooking, needlework, and carpentry are just a few such examples. A hobby that does not rely on other people makes it much easier to do and allows you to continue it indefinitely. Not only will you never have to wait for someone else to be available, but you'll get valuable reflection time alone. Do something that you really look forward to. Do something just for you.

Of course, you will also want a hobby that you *can* share with a friend or spouse. As they say, "People who play together, stay together." A hobby should feel like play. Dancing, chess, bowling, pool, and horseshoes are examples of hobbies to share with others. Save a little time for your hobbies every day or every week as time allows. Really get into your hobby. Let your passion grow for your hobbies. At the same time, let your hobbies give you passion.

Exercise is one of the best, least expensive things you can do for yourself. It diminishes tension, enhances your health, and improves your self-esteem. You can do it alone or with friends. Exercise also helps keep your weight under control and helps you look your best. No matter how busy you are, you must make room for exercise. Run, walk, play basketball, play softball, lift weights, but do something. Getting started in a

Exercise is one of the best, least expensive things you can do for yourself.

routine is the hard part. However, once you do, it will become a greatly anticipated part of your day. So if you haven't already, get started exercising. There are no excuses not to.

If you find an exercise program or hobby to help you unwind, your stress level will decrease and your effectiveness at work will increase. Coworkers will enjoy your company more because you will be less tense and more refreshed. Constructive, enjoyable downtime is a key component to successful hard work. Play hard so that you can work hard. And work hard so that you can play hard.

There are many stories of people who took their hobbies and created business opportunities for themselves. What a blessing it is when people supplement their income by doing something they had already enjoyed as fun. For example, Earl Suttle combined his love for sports and his talent for speaking to become a motivational speaker and consultant with the NBA and NFL. This did not happen overnight. It took planning, passion, and perseverance. When these forces work together, the payoff can be great. Is a merger of your passions and talent possible? Really think about it. Develop some creative ideas and give it a try.

* * * *

TRY THESE IDEAS:

1. Do you have a hobby activity to do at least once a week? If you don't, develop one that is right for you. Find one that you will really look forward to.

2. Think about what activities you want to do when you retire. If you want to travel, perhaps a photography hobby would work well. If you plan to stay put, perhaps painting or music is something you can begin to develop now.

* * * *

Suggested Affirmation: Say out loud 10 times, "I am doing more hobbies than ever before because it reduces my stress and gives me more energy to be productive on my job."

* * * *

Write down the most important thing(s) to remember from this Pearl:

_____

_____

_____

_____

PEARL # 27

Cherish Your Loved Ones and Your Pets

"Love God with all your heart and with all your soul and with all your mind. This is the first and greatest commandment. And the second is like it: Love your neighbor as yourself."
—Jesus Christ, *Matthew 22:37-39, Bible*

"Express appreciation to your loved ones earlier and often."
—John Maxwell

"The deepest principle in human nature is the craving to be appreciated."
—William James

* * * *

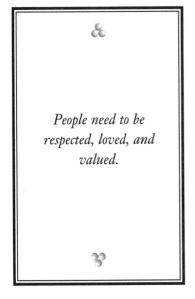

People need to be respected, loved, and valued.

MANY OF OUR PEARLS relate to finding purpose and successfully achieving your goals. We cannot neglect love. In no way can we neglect love. In fact, the Bible says, "God is love" (1 John 4:16). *People need to be respected, loved, and valued.* Who are the special people in your life? More importantly, how often are you taking time to express your love and appreciation to them? Sometimes people are very quick to express negative feelings and slow to convey the positive feelings they have. Your wife or husband, children, parents, grandparents, and grandchildren are all special people requiring your rich and unconditional love. There is something grand about caring grandparents. You can be the worst person in the world and they will still love you. You can hear them say, "Come here, honey, I'll hug you." They love you unconditionally. Family members, special friends, and even your pets—all need need warmth and caring.

Build loving relationships and cherish these relationships. Learn how to take good care of your wife or husband. People think love relationships are easy and come naturally. Learning more about caring for love relationships seems strange to some people. But there is evidence all around us that many people have more to learn. Just look at the high divorce rates in this country. Divorce has become so common that some people in our society think of it as the norm. They forget the special and spiritual nature of marriage as it was designed by God.

Nobody's saying it's easy, though. As the title of author John Gray's book says, "Men are from Mars and women are from Venus." Think about it. It's true. It often seems as though men and women are from different planets! The truth is, the genders *are* different. And because genders are so different, there is a lot to learn about one another. Husbands and wives must continuously learn about each other and strive to maintain (or perhaps recover) their closeness.

Of course, the examples of gender differences we have cited are just generalizations. Certainly, they do not apply to everyone. However, they do provide endless material for stand-up comedians and book writers. But left unexamined, our differences can cause real problems. We need to find ways to understand each other and, when appropriate, laugh at our differences. The point is to educate yourself about your partner. It will make a big difference in your happiness, in your relationships at home, and perhaps in your understanding of coworkers of the opposite gender.

Parents, cherish your children. They are special people given specifically to you. They grow up all too fast. Children teach parents a lot about love. Isn't it strange that the more you sacrifice for your children the more you love them? They bring you great joy and happiness with their smiles, laughs, and hugs. They are, or should be, the personification of the love in your marriage.

And children (six to sixty years old) should cherish their parents. As Jesus said, "…Honor your father and mother…" (Matthew 19:19). Your parents are not perfect but they probably sacrificed more for you than you can imagine. Unfortunately not everyone is blessed with a loving family. Changes in our society have thinned the ranks of stable families. Be determined, though, not to let your family become another societal casualty.

Not having your own children doesn't mean you can't care for and help children. Parents, teachers, aunts, uncles, counselors, and others can be a blessing to children. For those of you who have wonderful parents, be thankful. For those of you who did not have a supportive family, try to find forgiveness, faith, and helpful mentors. Also be true to God, your Heavenly Father. We live only a few short years in this world and will then be judged by God for our faith and actions. So don't wait to build your love relationship with God. It is the most important relationship you have.

Did you know your job is conditional? If you do good work, you may be able to stay. If not, you probably will not be there for a long. Many of your friendships are conditional too. They need nurturing, time, and understanding. Try not to neglect your friends. They require attention. Everyone needs unconditional support systems, too. Spouses, children, parents, brothers, sisters, and grandparents often are (or should be) a source of this unconditional love. Be sure you appreciate them for the love they give. Never take unconditional love for granted. It deserves better.

Another great unconditional support system is a pet. *Pets, too, can bring out love in people.* Not everyone has the time for a pet, but

Pets, too, can bring out love in people.

if you do they can be wonderful company. Research says that people who own pets actually live longer! Do you own a pet? Pets never talk back to you (unless, of course, you have a parrot). Moreover, pets don't care how rich or good-looking you are. They love you all the time! Dr. Hubbard is always amazed at the joy his daughter Tara's cats bring to her. No matter what her day was like, when "Pud" and "Pufffies" approach her, she smiles, relaxes, and happily pets them. To her, Pud is like a king; Puffies, likewise, gets the royal treatment of a princess. And any stray cat that Tara sees will be benefit from the emergency supply of cat food she keeps in the back of her car.

Dr. Hubbard's daughter, Erin, has brought home more animals than the Hubbard house could ever hold. Dogs, cats, rabbits, turtles, fish, and many others have captured her heart. One of Erin's cats named LBC (Little Black Cat) has an almost mystical gift of empathy: "sensing" when someone feels down, the cat offers purrs and love to the dejected. Equally interesting is LBC's insistence on standing in the face of anyone who happens to be singing. (A carolling enthusiast, LBC is perhaps happiest at Christmastime, when singing is commonplace in the Hubbard household.) God just seems to send animals to people so that their hearts will know more love. So long as you take decent care of them, pets—and their unconditional love—will always be there for you.

So take some time to build love relationships and friendships in your life. Take time because it's vital. Exercise your relationships like your exercise your body. Your job may be important, but later in life it will be the time you spent with your family that will mean the most to you.

* * * *

TRY THESE IDEAS:

1. Be involved in activities with your special people. Dancing, cards, and tennis are just a few examples.

2. Find out what makes your special people happy and give it to them. If you are not sure what makes them happy, what should you do? Ask them!

3. Have things outside your relationship that makes you okay with you. If you have good things outside your relationship, then you bring some good things to that relationship.

* * * *

Suggested Affirmation: Say out loud 10 times, "I am expressing my love, warmth, and concern for my loved ones every time I can."

* * * *

Write down the most important thing(s) to remember from this Pearl:

_____

_____

_____

_____

P E A R L # 2 8

If You Are Not Moving Forward, You Are Probably Moving Backwards

"If you are not moving forward, you are probably moving backwards."
—Dr. John Hubbard

"Never look back unless you want to go that way."
—Anonymous

"The real purpose to our existence is not to make a living, but to make a life. A worthy well rounded useful life by doing all the good you can by all the means you can, in all the ways you can to all the people you can, as long as ever you can."
—Anonymous

"If we all make a few little adjustments, it can bring the genius out in all of us."
—Albert Einstein

* * * *

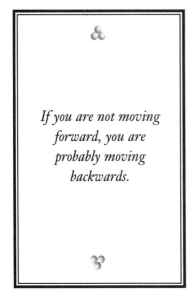

If you are not moving forward, you are probably moving backwards.

IN HIS SEMINARS, Earl often says the following: "I went to the edge of the cliff. I thought I might fall. I went to the edge of the cliff. I thought I might fall. I went to the edge of the cliff and somebody pushed me and ..." He allows the audience to complete the story out loud. Almost everyone says, "I fell." But a few say, "I flew!" His point with this story is that many people think that if they get pushed they will fall. However, when you are pushed you often become better, more challenged, and energized. Earl has audiences share their own stories about what occurred early in their lives when somebody or something pushed them. Slowly, one by one, they tell stories of success and admit that they had almost forgotten they were at their best when someone pushed them. *People need some pushing now and then to grow.*

The ability to find motivation and continue to learn is an important characteristic of successful people. Remember, if you are not moving forward, you are probably moving backwards! Think about that. It appears to be a law of nature. Once you stopped learning a foreign language in school, you began to forget it. It's true, isn't it? When you are not cleaning your house, it gets messier. Once you stop regular exercise, you begin to put on weight and lose muscle mass. If you are not adding to your knowledge, resources, health, spirit, and character, then these too will begin to diminish!

By now you should be moving forward in many areas of your life (if you have put into practice the Pearls we have already discussed). You should have a plan for success, be practicing techniques to build self-esteem, developing stronger support systems, and growing in your spiritual faith. You cannot be all things to all people, and you can't study quantum physics the rest of your life. In fact, who would want to? (Our apologies to quantum physicists.) But you can keep learning new and exciting things! You can continue to improve the "Big You." That is, keep improving your overall mind, body, and spirit. To do this you must keep challenging yourself to move forward by doing new things or improving your current status in each of these important areas.

Try some new things and vary what you already do. Cross-training is a great way to keep things fresh and get the most of your time. Those of you who exercise regularly know exactly what we are talking about. Doing the same exercise routine over and over again is boring and becomes less and less productive. In athletics, "cross-training" means that you vary your exercises to work on different muscle groups or the same muscle groups in new and different ways. Not only does it prevent boredom, but the varied muscle movements produce a greater overall benefit. For example, a person may mix in some swimming with his daily jogging routine; a golfer may want (or need) to play some tennis or jog occasionally. And weightlifters work on their chest and legs one day, and their biceps and abdominals the next. Be creative.

For a healthier life, try brisk walking, jogging, swimming, tennis or golfing with friends. Mix it up a bit. Even in the highly competitive world of professional sports an athlete may not peak in overall performance at the same time as his or her raw physical abilities peak. Instead, an athlete who gains experience and learns new techniques may peak

People need some pushing now and then to grow.

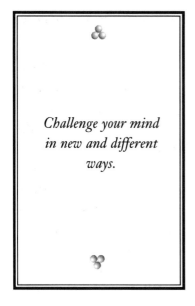

Challenge your mind in new and different ways.

later in their career. In fact, their "bigger self" may realize its best growth when their career is over and they find they have more time to give back to their family and community. As they say, "When one door is closed, others will open."

Challenge your mind in new and different ways. Pick up a little Spanish or French, learn to play the piano, or take up cooking lessons. Why not? What is stopping you? Don't worry about never becoming a fluent Spanish speaker or a concert violinist. Who cares? Find your passion. Read often and on different topics. Many people get so busy that they forget how enjoyable reading and learning can be. Perhaps you could go back to school or take a college course or two. Community colleges and adult education centers have much to offer. Accountants can enroll in an auto mechanics workshop and carpenters can take a class in finance. Enjoy the process of learning, meeting new people, and enhancing your personal growth.

Look into your heart and you will find many things you want to do and learn. Work on your mental versatility. Like other organs of your body, brain function declines over time. It gets old and rusty, too. Memory and sharpness diminish. However, many studies have shown that you can slow down that process by exercising your mind regularly, the same way exercising your muscles staves off atrophy. Instead of watching television sit-coms, consider the Discovery channel or the Learning channel. Learn to play the piano, take up painting, or perhaps develop your computer skills. These things not only keep you sharp, they make you a more interesting person. And don't use your age as an excuse not to try new things; you're never too old to learn.

Everyone approaches his or her spiritual growth a little differently. If you look at all the strange creatures in the world, it is obvious that God loves diversity! So search your heart and you will find ways to brighten your spiritual journey, too. In fact, this may be the most important change you ever make. Perhaps you will challenge yourself to read the Bible or another inspiring book. Perhaps you will decide to tithe, join a church, or a Bible study group. Spiritual growth may include getting out to help orphans or the homeless. How is your prayer life? Do you keep God in your life with regular prayer? It is your eternal spirit, so take good care of it. Many people put off working on their faith until they are senior citizens. There are, however, three problems with this approach. First, a healthy spiritual life will help you be your best throughout your life. It will enhance your happiness, productivity, and family life now. It will help guard you from making bad mistakes. Second, it allows you to help others grow spiritually (including your children and spouse). It would be a shame to wait until you have very few years left to help others spiritually. And finally, no one knows if they will be alive tomorrow, much less years from now. The Bible contains a parable about a man who worked very hard, creating a stockpile of goods so that he'd never have to work in his later years. What the man did not know, however, was that he would in fact die the day after he finished collecting his goods. So don't wait to grow in your faith. Search for answers and direction now.

If you're not continually learning and growing, other people will pass you by. If you do not keep growing you will keep deteriorating! It is nice to know that while a decline in some areas cannot be stopped all together, other areas of health, knowledge, and spirit can be sustained. So remember, if you are not moving forward, you will soon be moving backwards.

* * * *

TRY THESE IDEAS:

1. Decide to learn to play a musical instrument or new ways to use your computer.

2. Buy a book that is spiritually inspiring. Buy it today. You will forget to do it if you wait until next week. The Bible is a great place to start.

3. Decide to challenge your body. Loose weight, run, or build some muscle mass. Join the YMCA or another gym if you don't belong to one.

* * * *

Suggested Affirmation: Say out loud 10 times, "I am challenging myself every day in order to keep growing."

* * * *

Write down the most important thing(s) to remember from this Pearl:

_____

_____

_____

_____

PEARL # 29

&

Keep Learning

"Getting old is great as long as you are growing."
—Vincent Price

"What we have to learn to do, we learn by doing."
—Aristotle

*"Education is simply the soul of a society as it
passes from one generation to another."*
—G.H. Chesterton

* * * *

MOST PEOPLE READING THIS BOOK have probably completed their formal education. That is fine. However, that does not mean you stop making major efforts to learn. Have a student's heart as long as you live. Learning keeps you young. As Dr. Howard Hendricks has said, "As long as you live, you learn; and as long as you learn, you live." *No matter how old you are, never stop learning.* Henry Ford said, "Anyone who stops learning is old, whether at twenty or eighty. Anyone who keeps learning stays young."

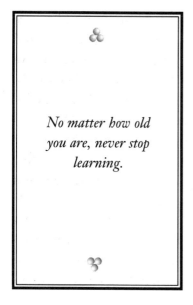

No matter how old you are, never stop learning.

Have you ever known people who are really talented but never seem to become successful? Perhaps you've met people with high IQ's but low grades. Others have wonderful athletic gifts, but don't really help the team. There are many different reasons why people underachieve. Unwillingness to learn from others is one that is a prime example. Some underachievers may not listen to their parents, boss, teacher, or coach. Refusing to learn from those who would teach you is a big mistake. Some people just think they know it all already. In fact, many teenagers believe they know it all before the age of 16! What could parents and teachers possibly teach them? Perhaps they were told they have a high IQ or got all A's in high school. Perhaps they have developed a bad habit of looking down on people. Instead of being thankful for their gift and learning all they can, it sometimes goes to their head and they stop learning. And when they stop learning, they become unproductive. What a waste!

As unfortunate as this is, the good news is that this condition is easily reversed. After all, learning from others is the reason that people read books. The fact that you are examining yourself through this book is a very good sign. To have a high IQ or straight A's doesn't mean a person knows everything. In fact, all it really means is that they're more adept at learning, provided they have teachers and the right attitude. How many times have you seen a person with less natural intelligence/talent surpass a more talented person because of the former's attitude of learning? It happens all the time!

There are two kinds of people we need to learn from. There are those who are successful and those who are failures. It is too bad that people who are failures don't write books more often or give more seminars. They have a lot to teach. Sometimes, they can be our best teachers. Earl is a seminar leader at the NBA Rookie Transition Program, in which veteran and former NBA players speak to the rookies. Although the rookies enjoy what the successful veterans have to say, they tend to pay even more attention to former players who have destroyed their careers. Suddenly there is a shift in the energy level of the room, when a player who has made some serious mistakes is speaking. Almost every one of the rookies sits up and listens intently. They earnestly take notes. They hang on every word. Some even fight back tears as they listen to the sad stories of talented players whose bad choices led them down a path of disaster. Fearful that such a fate could befall them, the rookies become earnest students of these former NBA players.

Still, it can be much easier and far more fun to learn from outstanding examples. Be with successful people, learn from them, and read about those you can't be with. People in history are fascinating, and biographies are wonderful teaching tools. You can't speak to Gandhi, George Washington Carver, or Albert Einstein, but by reading about them you can still learn from them. Go to courses, seminars, and lectures. The Bible is another book to learn from. It is both a book of faith and of history. *No one is too smart or too great to learn from the Bible.*

Everyone is different and has something a little unique to teach you. Learn from people around you

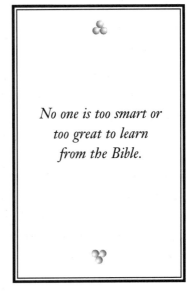

No one is too smart or too great to learn from the Bible.

who have been successful. Be like a sponge and absorb new ideas. And don't get bored by something just because you have already heard it. Old concepts can be seen with new perspectives. Some books, like the Bible, can be read over and over and continually offer new insights. You may miss something the first time around because you're not ready for a particular lesson. Later, when you have the proper background, that which you'd previously read takes on a whole new meaning.

The library is a great place at the right price. Everything there is free for the asking. You only need your (free) library card. Books and tapes are enjoyable and can change your life. As British writer Richard Steele said, "Reading is to the mind what exercise is to the body."

We suggest a varied list; read biographies, self-help books, as well as fictional stories. A single book can change your life. Are you reading (or listening) to the books that are going to take you where you need to be five, ten, or twenty years from now? We are thankful you are reading this one, but you will need to read others as well. Stay inspired to read and grow. Start a personal library. You might not think your busy schedule allows time to read, but try to find a way to make the time. Some people listen to audiobooks while they drive. This is especially good for people with long commutes who have little time for reading at home. Dr. Hubbard generally has a biography, motivational tape, and fictional novel audiotape in his car at all times. In this way he can tune into whatever area of learning he feels like. Take a moment and search your heart for what type of book you need in your life right now. Charles Jones said, "Not one of you five years from now will be any different than you are today except for the books that you read and people that you associate with." Read that quote again and think about the importance of that statement!

Are you growing and finding meaning in what you do? There are many books that have helped people find meaning in their lives. An example of a book we highly recommend is *The Richest Man in Babylon* by George Clason. This is a financial book that is easy to find and easy to read. It is told in short story form and you can probably get through it in one night. Financial problems are all too common. That one book may change your financial philosophy and increase your income. Another great financial book is *Think and Grow Rich* by Napoleon Hill. His message is simple and powerful. Basically he says to know what you want and don't give up until you get it. An excellent psychology book-on-tape is *The Psychology of Achievement* by Brian Tracy. In his book, techniques are discussed for stress reduction, performance enhancement, and better control of your emotions. And we would be remiss not to suggest John Gray's *Men are from Mars and Women are from Venus* or Susan Taylor' *Lessons for Living* for help with your relationships. There are many others we highly recommend. Take a look at our bibliography to get more ideas.

Reading is an important habit to continually fuel you with new ideas and information that you can bring to your work, your homes, and the golf course.

Reading is an important habit to continually fuel you with new ideas and information that you can bring to your work, your homes, and the golf course. In all the ways you can, KEEP LEARNING! It is a great way to grow and to take control of your life's direction. As the old saying goes, "A mind is a terrible thing to waste." And as William James has said, "It's never to late to become what you want to become."

* * * *

TRY THESE IDEAS:

1. Identify the biggest stress in your life. Is it money, rela-
    tionships, sex, kids? Find a good book on the subject and
    learn.

2. Ask a friend you respect what book has been their great-
    est inspiration. Get it and read it.

3. Listen to inspirations or fun tapes whenever you go on
    a long drive by yourself. You will be hooked in no time.

* * * *

Suggested Affirmation: Say out loud 10 times, "I am learning
more, earning more, and giving back more because I know the
importance of learning."

* * * *

**Write down the most important thing(s) to remember from
this Pearl:**

_____

_____

_____

_____

PEARL # 30

Never Quit

"I have not yet begun to fight."
—John Paul Jones, U.S. Naval Hero

"You may be whatever you resolve to be."
—General "Stonewall" Jackson

"When one door of happiness closes, another opens."
—Helen Keller

* * * *

W E SAVED THIS PEARL FOR LAST because it is probably the most important one. *If your dreams and goals are really worth achieving, never quit until you have achieved them.* As Zig Ziglar has said, "It's not where you start—It's where you finish that counts." *Your level of success, achievement, and excellence will correlate more with a philosophy of never quitting than perhaps any other.* Determination, resolve, and commitment are the cornerstones of successful people. As Samuel Johnson said, "Great works are performed not by strength, but by perseverance." A person must never quit if the road they are on is right.

If your dreams and goals are really worth achieving, never quit until you have achieved them.

There is an often told story of Winston Churchill's greatest speech. He was asked to address a grade school audience. The principal instructed all the children to come with their notebooks and pencil, and be prepared to take a lot of notes. When Winston Churchill got up to speak he said, "Never, ever give up." He then sat down. Everyone sat quietly, thinking he would get back up and talk some more. But he never did. It was probably his greatest speech. Winston Churchill led Great Britain through their most dangerous time in World War II. And after all that he went through, what was his message to these young people? "Never, ever give up." What else was there to say?

You need to know where you are going and why. Most people don't know where they are, where they are going, or why they want to get there. Hopefully, you made those determinations as you worked through the previous Pearls in this book. You have goals, dreams, and plans. You must also be hard-working and never give up. Life will throw surprises and road blocks at you, but so what. Life throws curve balls at everyone. This is earth, not heaven. Use your plan and take appropriate action to get around

Your level of success, achievement, and excellence will correlate more with a philosophy of never quitting than perhaps any other.

your problems. After you set that plan and direction into play, never quit. Like ants, never quit.

People that plow through adversity are the people most respected. Don't you admire people who never quit? Napoleon Hill's great book *Think and Grow Rich* gives some wonderful examples of how very successful people broke down all barriers to achieve financial success. We suggest that you read that book or listen to the tape. The key to their success was never quitting. Gandhi was a great example of a man who did not quit while trying against great odds to achieve his dream for India's freedom. He freed India from British domination by his sheer courage and determination. Likewise, George Washington is not necessarily regarded as a great general, but he was a great leader in many people's eyes. By sheer perseverance he kept his revolutionary army together for eight long years, which led to the birth of the USA. The determination you admire in others is the determination you must cultivate in yourself.

Watch a couple "Rocky" movies sometime. What did Rocky have that the others didn't, besides one heck of a strong jaw? He was hit over and over again. Rocky did not even have much boxing talent. So what made him special? HE DIDN'T GIVE UP. No matter how often he was hit, he kept coming back. If he got knocked down, he got back up. Why were the Rocky movies such a huge success? They were box office hits because they told people a message they instinctively knew they needed to hear! It was a message of hope, courage, and determination. Sure, the tales of Rocky Balboa are only movies, but millions of real people live determined lives everyday. You may want to read a book about an Alabama woman named Helen Keller. Helen Keller could not hear, speak, or see, and yet she achieved enormous success. You can find countless stories about people overcoming bankruptcy, severe illness, and personal loss because they had the WILL to do so.

How long should you work on improving important areas of your life like your health, marriage, relationship with your children, education, financial security, and relationship with God? AS LONG AS IT TAKES! How long? AS LONG AS IT TAKES!

What if you had an "I'll never give up" attitude? You'd be a huge success, wouldn't you? Marriages would not fail. People would develop successful businesses and careers. Humanitarians would see that their communities obtained needed resources such as parks and playgrounds. You would be confident and successful. What could stop you? Who could stop you? What's the problem with most people today? They give up too soon, don't they? That's why so many people don't flourish and instead settle for much less than their potential. You may need to adjust your strategies and your plan, but not the determination to achieve your dream (if it is truly worthwhile). So have an exciting dream. Develop a plan to achieve your dream, build your resources, and NEVER, EVER GIVE UP.

* * * *

TRY THESE IDEAS:

1. Re-clarify your goals and dreams.
2. If your dream(s) is a good one, a right one, be resolved never to give up on it. Write it down to remind you of your direction. Read it often.

* * * *

Suggested Affirmation: Say out loud 10 times, "I am always bouncing back like a tennis ball. I will never ever give up on my dreams."

* * * *

Write down the most important thing(s) to remember from this Pearl:

_____

_____

_____

_____

Addendum

THANK YOU FOR READING THIS BOOK. We hope you enjoyed it and got some helpful ideas. If you forget all else, we want you to remember one thing, the "TAP Principle" for excellence:

Step 1 — TRUST

Step 2 — ATTITUDE & ACTION

Step 3 — PASSION & PERSEVERANCE

* * * *

God bless you!

Bibliography and Suggested Reading

Alessander, Tony and O'Conner, J., *People Smarts*, Jossey-Bass Pfreffer, 1994.

Bach, David, *Smart Women Finish First Rich*, Broadway Book, 1999.

Bramson, Robert, *Coping with Difficult People*, A Dell Book, 1981.

Branden, Nathaniel, *Six Pillars of Self Esteem*, Bantam Books, 1995.

Brown, Les, *Live Your Dreams*, William Norron Co, 1992.

Chandler, Steve, *100 Ways to Motivate Yourself*, Bookmart Press, 2001.

Chopra, Deepak, *The Seven Spiritual Laws of Success*, Amber-Allen Publishing, 1995.

Clason, George, *The Richest Man In Babylon*, New American Library, 1955.

Cook, John, *The Book of Positive Quotations*, Fairview Press, 1993.

Convey, Stephen, *Seven Habits of Highly Effective People*, Simon and Schuster, 1989.

Covey, Stephen, *Principle-Centered Leadership*, Simon and Schuster, 1990.

Drucker, Peter, *The Effective Executive*, Harper Business, 1993.

Elder, Richard, *If I Knew Then What I Know Now*, Berkley Publishing, 1996.

Gray, John, *Men Are From Mars, Women Are From Venus*, Harper Collins, 1992.

Harrell, Keith, *Attitude is Everything*, Cliff Street Book, 2002.

Hendricks, Howard, *Teaching to Change Lives*, Bullentine, 1976.

Hubbard, John and Albanese, Robert (Eds), *Primary Care Medicine for Specialists and Non-specialists*, Kluwer Acedemic/Plenum Publishers, 2002.

Hubbard, John and Short, Delmer (Eds), *Primary Care Medicine for Psychiatrist*, Plenum Press, 1992.

Hubbard, John, *The Handbook of Stress Medicine*, CRC Press, 1997.

Hubbard, John and Workman, Edward (Eds), *Substance Abuse in the Mentally and Physically Disabled*, Marcel Dekker, Inc., 2001.

Kehoe, John, *Mind Power in the 21st Century*, 2002.

Kiyosaki, Robert and Lechter, Sharon, *Rich Dad, Poor Dad*, Warner Books, 1997.

MacMillan Dictionary of Quotations, Chartwell Books, Random House, 2000.

Maxwell, John, *Developing the Leader Within*, Thomas Nelson Publishing, 2001.

Maxwell, John, *Failing Forward*, Thomas Nelson Publishing, 2001.

Mellott, Roger, *Stress Management for Professionals*, (audiotape) Career Truck Publications, 1991.

McKay, Harvey, *Swim With the Sharks Without Being Eaten Alive*, (audiotape) Bantam Books-Audio, 1989.

Neibuhr, Reinhold, *Serenity Prayer*, 1926.

Oakley, Ed and Krug, Doug, *Enlightened Leadership*, Simon and Schuster, 1991.

Orman, Suze, *The 9 Steps to Financial Freedom*, (audiotape) Random House, 1997.

Peters, Thomas and Waterman, Robert, *In Search of Excellence*, Harper and Row, 1982.

Peck, Scott, *The Road Less Traveled*, Simon and Schuster, 1978.

Rennolds, Joyce, *Energy Connection*, JR Publishing, 2002.

Ries, Al and Trout, Jack, *Positioning*, Warner Books, 1986.

Robinson, Edwin Arlington, "Richard Cory," in *Collected Poems*, MacMillan Company, 1921.

Rohn, Jim, *Art of Exceptional Living*, Simon and Schuster, 1994.

Salsburg, Glenna, *Passion, Power and Purpose*, (audiotape) Salsburg Enterprises, 1989.

Suttle, Felicia, *Dare to Dream, Black and White* Publications, 1999.

Taylor, Susan, *Lesson in Living*, Random House, 1998.

Thichy, Noel, *Leadership Engine*, Harper Business, 1997.

Thomspson, *Chain Reference Bible* (New International Version), Kirkbride Bible Co.

Tracy, Brian, *The Psychology of Achievement*, Simon and Schuster, 1994.

Vanzant, Iyanla, *Acts of Faith, Daily Mediations for People of Color*, Simon and Schuster, 1993.

Williamson, Marianne, *A Return to Love (reflections) on the Principles of a Course in Miracles*, Harper Collins Publishing, 1992.

*   *   *   *

Notes & Ideas

Notes & Ideas

Notes & Ideas

Notes & Ideas

Notes & Ideas

Notes & Ideas

Do you know someone who could benefit from a copy of this book?

Perhaps it is your son or daughter, husband or wife, friend or co-worker.

ORDER NOW!

EARL'S PEARLS ON ENJOYING EXCELLENCE

ORDER FORM

Name: _____

Address: _____

City/State/Zip: _____

Daytime Phone: _____ E-mail : _____

Quantity	Item Description		Price	Total
	Earl's Pearls on Enjoying Excellence	Soft Cover	$17.95	
		Hard Cover	$24.95	

Shipping and Handling (Continental USA)
(Additional for International orders.)

Up to $36.00 .... add $5.50
$37.00 – $49.99 .... add $7.50
$50.00 – $99.99 .... add $9.50
Over $100.00 .... add $11.50

Please note: When ordering 5 or more books, the following discount prices apply:
Soft cover–$15.00 • Hard cover – $20.00

Add Total of Items _____

Add Shipping and Handling _____

Add Sales Tax _____
(Soft cover $1.25 per book)
(Hard cover $1.75 per book)

Total Enclosed (US funds only) _____

Personal Check: *Make payable to Victory International Publishers (VIP)*

❏ Master Card   ❏ Visa   ❏ Amercan Express   ❏ Discover

Card #: _____/_____/_____/_____   Exp:_____/_____

(Print) Name: _____ Signature: _____

City: _____ State:_____ Zip:_____

Phone: _____ Fax: _____ E-mail : _____

❏ My company is interested in hosting an Earl Suttle Seminar

Mail all orders to:

VICTORY INTERNATIONAL PUBLISHERS
920 Renaissance Way • Roswell, GA 30076
Phone: 770-650-0399 • Fax: 770-650-9666 • E-mail: earl@earlsuttle.com
www.earlsuttle.com

231